SEVEN FRIENDS

To
My Daughter Deirdre

LOUIS MARLOW

Seven Friends

LONDON
THE RICHARDS PRESS
No. 8 Charles II Street
St. James's Square
1953

Acknowledgments with thanks are due: to Mr. Vyvyan Holland for permission to include letters of Oscar Wilde: to Mr. John Cowper Powys and John Lane the Bodley Head for permission to quote from the Autobiography *of John Cowper Powys: to Mr. T. F. Powys and Messrs. Chatto & Windus for permission to quote from the works of T. F. Powys: to Miss Alyse Gregory and John Lane the Bodley Head for permission to quote from the works of Llewelyn Powys. Also to the following for permission to draw from my essays published by them: on Frank Harris in* World Review *(Edward Hulton): on The Brothers Powys in* Essays by Divers Hands XXIV *(The Royal Society of Literature): on Friends and Friendship in* The Pleasure Ground *(Messrs. Macdonald & Co.): on Somerset Maugham in* Writers of To-day *(Messrs. Sidgwick & Jackson).*

L.M.

LONDON: THE RICHARDS PRESS LTD
MARTIN SECKER: DIRECTOR

Contents

OSCAR WILDE

THERE is one thing at least of which there should be no complaint in our "sad, late day", and that is the changed view of Oscar Wilde. When I was a Cambridge undergraduate in 1904 one of the dons—I think the metaphysician MacTaggart — remarked that Wilde had now ceased to be an unspeakable blackguard and become an unfortunate man of genius. We have gone further on than that: "unfortunate man of genius" hardly covers the ground today. Wilde is not, as he was soon after his death, an object of pity; his sufferings, his tragedy, are too long past. It is his glamour to which there is now a more general response than ever before. To the fascination of the figure that he cut in his period, to his unique interest as a person, there is a susceptibility that increases. Book after book is written about him and they have large sales. One reason for this may be that his life and his writings satisfy a nostalgia for the life of the later nineteenth century as no other life and writings do. The way of his life, the way of the lives of the people in his plays that are so often revived—what a treat for us today, young and old, to look at that pattern of living! All the same, the younger ones can never

I

respond to the great Oscar as those of my age can, those who were subject in our youth to the special spell of the man as he then was, living still in tragic isolation among what seemed the ruins of his fame. Men and women older than myself, who remember the years before his fall, will say that we who were children in 1895 cannot have the full response that they have, and no doubt they are right. But mine contents me, it is no less satisfying, though it is naturally less excitingly rebellious than it was in my youth. It is, also naturally, less uncritical. How odd that the man whom the Victorians persecuted and tortured should have had so many outstanding Victorian qualities: sentimentalism, mawkishness, melodrama, religiosity, moral humbug. Witness the plays—except of course the surely immortal masterpiece *The Importance of Being Earnest*—the poems, and, above all, *De Profundis* and *The Ballad of Reading Gaol*. The worst humbug and the worst mawkishness are in these two last, both written after he was sent to prison, which shows what a bad effect punishment can have.

But what an incomparable figure! What a magnet! What golden wit and spirit and sense! No wonder that the most normal young men of the *fin-de-siècle*, if susceptible to charm of personality, to genius of conversation, to the exciting magic of words, should have done their level best to become homosexuals merely to do him honour. How good and satisfying to think that the judge who passed upon him a sentence accompanied by the most atrocious imaginable moral cant, is entirely forgotten, and that Wilde is more famous than ever.

That kind of moral cant is now unfashionable, but the laws making homosexuality criminal are still in force. In such matters we are subject to minority rule because of the cowardice of the majority. I doubt if more than a quite small minority, most of whom are probably suppressed homosexuals, now want to put homosexuals in prison. Most people regard them as a rather amusing variation; jokes are publicly made about them, even so publicly as in plays and revues and comic " turns ". And indeed they are amusing, often witty themselves as well as " the cause that wit is in others "; with a wit and a humour peculiarly their own; a shadow, at least, sometimes, of Oscarian wit and humour. I remember the indignant retort made by one of them to the suggestion that he should for a change pay attention to a certain Lesbian: " But, my dear, I'm a perfectly normal woman! " which may, on the distaff side, be matched by the reply to the marriage proposal " I want you for my wife: " " I didn't know you were married."

Why, I wonder, can't we leave these people alone? As they do in the Latin and Scandinavian countries. Russian reversion to this kind of punitive interference should be a popular and respectable argument against it.

It is Nature's way to throw up abnormalities,

3

she has done this from the beginning and so she will continue. Harmful abnormalities should be cured, if they can be, and, if not, killed; but the average homosexual is harmless, he cannot corrupt, he can convert only the converted. He cannot be cured, because he no more wants to be cured than we others want to be cured of our heterosexuality, which is as unnatural to him as homosexuality is to us. Let us then be tolerant, all the more so when we reflect that the more homosexuals, the less competition in our own field.

More tolerant, at least, we are: general opinion, as so often happens, is ahead of legal and religious tabus. In 1895 the arrest of Oscar Wilde spread throughout England a strong, vindictive fury; there was a broadcasting of malignant rage that would not be possible now. Enlightenment has gradually spread, thanks to the efforts of such wise and humane men as Edward Carpenter and Havelock Ellis. And, now that natural instincts are less severely suppressed, there is less hidden envy of homosexual indulgence and so less desire to punish it.

I was only thirteen at the time of Wilde's trial and knew nothing about it. Perhaps because it was " that dreadful time when we had to hide away the newspapers," as one of my elders observed a few years later, thus imputing to Wilde the further crime of introducing obscene

4

reading matter into Victorian homes. Certainly he added then a new obscene word to the English language—his own Christian name. During the summer holidays of 1895 I remember my sister innocently saying that she thought the Oscar Wilde case was for breach of promise: Regina versus a Wilde who had jilted her. I didn't take much interest in that. It was not until about two years later that Oscar began to fascinate me; to stimulate me with an interest that grew the more absorbing as I came to realise fully the horror in which grown up people held him. Of course! What stronger satisfaction to a rebellious adolescent than the championship of " that monster of unspeakable vice " as " the poet victim of a cruel and unjust fate ". " I cannot but think of your cruel and unjust fate whenever I pass through Reading on my way to Radley " was what I wrote in my first schoolboy letter to Oscar Wilde.

He did not answer that letter. So I resorted to a ruse. I wrote again to him, inventing an " Ipswich Dramatic Society " of which I was Secretary, and asking permission to dramatise *The Picture of Dorian Gray* for performance by the members. That worked. Wilde replied, consenting, and this was the beginning of a correspondence that irradiated my youth and was one of its greatest excitements for the next two years.

Wilde told Robert Ross that I was the first stranger who had written to him sympathetically after his imprisonment. " He tells me," wrote

Wilde to Ross, " that he attended the *première* of *Lady Windermere's Fan*. I suppose he came in a perambulator." I had not attended that performance: I lied about it as I had lied about the Ipswich Dramatic Society. Any means was justified by the end of having Oscar as a correspondent. I cannot regret my lies that were rewarded by letters that are impressed, as almost all Wilde's letters are, however casually, with his " image and superscription ".

Certainly (he wrote from the Hotel d'Alsace, Paris, in reply to my letter about *Dorian Gray*) you can dramatise my play (*sic*)—but please tell me if the version is yours—and how the play is constructed.

Who acts Dorian Gray? He should be beautiful.

My work is so far in your hands that I rely on your artistic instinct that the play should have some quality of beauty and style.

You can have four performances, and if there should be any notices of the play in the papers pray let me see them.

Your letter of last summer gave me great pleasure—pray let me know all about yourself— who you are? What are you doing or going to do? Send me yr photograph.

Write to me at the above address—and direct the envelope to Sebastian Melmoth—a fantastic name that I shall explain to you some day.

At the end of the same year, 1898, he wrote from the Hotel des Bains, Napoule:

Thank you so much for your long and interesting letter: I envy you going to Oxford: it is the most flowerlike time of one's life—one sees the shadows of things in silver mirrors—later one sees the Gorgon's head, and one suffers, because it does not turn one to stone.

I am on the Riviera—in blue and gold weather —the sun warm as wine, and apricot-coloured: the little hotel where I am staying is right on the Golfe du Juan—and all round are pinewoods with their pungent breath: the wind growing aromatic as it moves through the branches: one's feet crushing sweetness out of the fallen needles. I wish you were here.

In your second letter you tell me that you enclose your photograph for me—but no photograph was in the letter! Your thoughts must have been in the crystal of the moon—call them back and let me have your portrait.

From the same hotel at Napoule he wrote, in February, 1899:

Your photographs arrived quite safely. I don't much like the amateur one—it makes you look far too old, and a little too learned: but in the other you have the eyes of the poet, and your hair is charming. I am sure it is shot with wonderful lights—and I like the curve of its curl. William Morris, in his translation of the Odyssey, renders " hyacinth-like hair " as " curled like the rings of the daffodil "—I remember—so perhaps that describes your curl.

Your last poem is most dainty in metre and treatment—I see you are studying the delicate *forms* of verse. That is quite right. To master one's instrument is the great thing. The " Circe " I like too, for its colour and passion—but in form it is not quite so good.

I hope you will devote yourself, with vows, to poetry. It is a sacramental thing, and there is no pain like it.

The gift of *The Importance of Being Earnest* a month or two later was an intoxicating joy, for which I offered a thanksgiving in the Radley Chapel:

I am sending you a book of mine—when it comes out—in about three weeks—you will get it. It is a fanciful, absurd comedy—written when I was playing with that Tiger, Life. I hope it will amuse you.

I am directing this to Radley—I suppose you are back there, educating the masters. Write to me soon. Your friend O.

The next letter came soon afterwards. Instead of using the formal " Mr." he now begins " My

8

Dear Boy ", and ends " Affectionately yours "
instead of " Sincerely ".

I am glad the play arrived safely, and has
amused you. It is quite irresponsible, but some
of the *obiter dicta* amuse *me*, and it was delightfully
acted.

I am, as you see, in Switzerland: on the Lake
of Geneva in the villa of a friend: across the
Lake, on the other side, are the mountains of
Savoy, and Mont Blanc: who at sunset flushes
like a rose: with shame perhaps at the prevalence
of tourists: he has lost all his terrors: spinsters
climb him now: and his snows are not virgin any
more.

The fringes of the Lake are fledged with pines,
but I don't like Switzerland: it has produced
nothing but theologians and waiters. Amiel
and Obermann are types of sterility: I attribute
it all to the lack of physical beauty in the race:
they are shapeless, colourless; grey of texture,
and without form: the beautiful races are the
great races: here they are like cavemen: no
impulse born of the splendour of physical per-
fection has ever filled them; their cattle have
more expression. Je m'ennuie, je m'ennuie.

So you love Shakespeare's Sonnets: I have
loved them, as one should love all things, not
wisely, but too well. In an old *Blackwood*—of I
fancy 1889—you will find a story of mine called
" The Portrait of Mr. W.H.", in which I have
expressed a new theory about the wonderful lad
whom Shakespeare so deeply loved. I think it

was the boy who acted in his plays. If you come across the story, read it, and tell me what you think.

So you knew Fitzgerald? His Omar is a masterpiece of art. I feel proud that a kinsman of mine—Sir Ralph Ouseley—brought the first M.S. of Omar Khayám to England: to Europe perhaps: it is the beautiful Bodleian M.S. which I suppose you have seen.

I had not pretended that I knew Edward Fitzgerald, who died when I was about a year old. My father knew him and I have been told that he patted me on my infant head. I don't think I mentioned this to Oscar, though I must have said something about his living near us or being an acquaintance of my father's.

In the summer of 1899 there was a postcard in French: from L'Ile d'Amour on the Marne:

Monsieur Sebastian Melmoth trouve votre sonnet très, très beau; et il espère reçevoir une autre lettre de vous prochainement.

Back at the Hotel d'Alsace, Paris, he writes in the following November:

Thanks so much, my dear boy, for your

photographs—they interest me, fascinate me much; not merely because they show me *you*, as you are, but because they show me what *I* was in my Oxford days—I have photographs of myself just like—so like that many of my friends think on seeing your photographs that they are of me—twenty years ago—the hair—the brow— the eyes—all strangely like—the suggestion charms me—but *you* must not, in life at any rate, trail purple palls of tragedy, or be caught in evil nets of Fate.

I like your poem " To — " very much: the one " with a moral " much less—Have you read " Jaspar Tristram " ? published by Heinemann— it is about Radley obviously—there are two boys in it—one of them like you to look at—the other like you to listen to—our age is full of mirrors and masks—if you have not read the book, order it— The early part—half Hellenic—is charming.

It was only two or three years ago that I saw what I think is as yet an unpublished letter of Wilde in which he tells his friend that the photo- graph that I sent him is " most beautiful "; and I do not mention this only out of vanity, but because it is amusing and so like Oscar that he should have written to me at the same time that this photograph was just like himself at that age. I wonder what he would have thought if he could have known that I was to be three times married.

The novel *Jaspar Tristram* is now forgotten:

but it is important as the first of the modern realistic public school stories, precursor of *The Loom of Youth* and very many others.

Later in the same month he wrote:

My Dear Boy, Do send me your new photograph. Did you ever receive a copy of my last play—" An Ideal Husband "? I told my publisher to send you one to Radley—I wrote your name on the title-page.

I think your poem " Hyacinthe "—(I don't like the longer title) very beautiful indeed: a most delicate work of art.

I am afraid you are going to be a poet—how tragic! how terribly tragic! In the waters of Helicon there is death—the only death worth dying. Affectionately yours Oscar.

That copy of *An Ideal Husband* must have gone astray; but he sent me another, inscribed " In recognition ". The " longer title " of the poem he refers to was *Hyacinthe et l'Amoureuse*: it is not surprising that he preferred " Hyacinthe " *tout court*. Of course he flattered me grossly about the verse that I sent him: it had no value. But no doubt he would have praised any verse by any boy whose letters and whose photographs he liked.

The next two letters—of January and February,

1900—were written just after I was eighteen and had left Radley.

I am very glad you have met my Australian friend—he is a charming fellow. Remember me to him—

So you are coming abroad—I think it is an admirable idea—Radley has nothing left to teach you—tho' you could have taught it much: did so, I doubt not.

I fear you would not like my hotel—I live there because I have no money ever—it is an absurd place: it is not a background. The only thing really nice in the whole Hotel is your own photograph: but one cannot, or one should not, play Narcissus to a photograph—even water is horribly treacherous: the eyes of one who loves one are the only mirror.

You asked me about " Melmoth ". Of course I have not changed my name: in Paris I am as well known as in London: it wd be childish.

But to prevent postmen having fits—I sometimes have my letters inscribed with the name of a curious novel by my Grand-Uncle, Maturin: a novel that was part of the romantic revival of the early century—and though imperfect—a pioneer—it is still read in France and Germany: Bentley republished it some years ago. I laugh at it, but it thrilled Europe—and is played as a play in modern Spain. Write soon. Your friend Oscar.

The next letter was addressed to Brussels where I was at a tutor's:

I am so glad that we are seemingly quite close to each other—at any rate without the " salt unplumbed estranging sea " between us— I hope you are perfecting yourself in French—to read Greek and speak French are two of the greatest pleasures in the cultivation of life.

If you have not read Georges Eekhoud's books —he is a Flamand—order them at once—" Mes Confessions ", and " Le Siècle Patibulaire ". The last has a wonderful story dedicated to me.

Could you come to Paris for a few days? Do, if you can.

I am very sorry that you are in correspondence with —. He is a most infamous young swindler, who selected *me*—of all ruined people—to swindle out of money: he is clever, but little more than a professional thief. He introduced himself to me, and induced me to make myself responsible for his Hotel bills—left me to pay them, and stole money besides—what the French call " un sale individu ". Don't write to him any more—or know him—but how *did* you know him? Please tell me by return—

I hope you have read Paul Adam's " Basile et Sophie "—a coloured Byzantine novel—very terrible—and curious: also get a little book called " Memoirs d'un petit Gendelettre " with a wonderful preface by Paul Adam. The author —Maurice Léon—committed suicide some months ago because he found that one could rarely speak the truth about others, never about oneself. He is a strange intellectual martyr— one who died not for Faith but for Doubt.

Also, do come to Paris. I am ill and unhappy

—the touch of your hand might heal me—
Always affectionately Oscar.
I am so glad you have found out my name.

At last I had ventured to address him by his
Christian name. He had been signing his
letters " Oscar " for some time.

I could not escape to Paris from the care of my
tutor. For one thing I hadn't enough money;
but during the summer of 1900 I was at Dieppe
with a laxer guardian so was at last in a position
to accept Oscar's invitation to come and see him.
But I would not for long be so fortunately placed.
My father and mother were very soon joining me,
and, anticipating some difficulty in gaining their
consent to my visit to Oscar, I was determined to
bring it off before their arrival. The letter that
follows, of July, 1900, threw me into an excess of
excited anticipation:

Come and see me next week—I can get you a
room in my Hotel.
I am not going to write to you any more—I
want to see you—I have waited long enough.

When all was arranged—the day, the hour of
departure—a telegram brought bitter disappoint-
ment. " Ne venez pas cette semaine je suis très
malade je vous ecrirai. Oscar." It was a heavy
blow.

He did not write again and we never met. About four months later he died. Robert Ross told me that Wilde telegraphed because he was afraid of disillusioning me. As he was then, ageing, in poor health, drinking too much, his distinction frayed, his good looks gone, he shrank from meeting a boy admirer who no doubt thought of him as he was in his heyday, the young Oscar, courted and commanding, the brilliant wit, the lovely poet. This explanation seems most likely to be the right one.

In a book recently published it appears that W. E. Henley tried to arrange a meeting between Wilde and myself on my seventh birthday; but I cannot lay claim to such precocity. As the meeting arranged more than eleven years later did not happen, I was a friend of Oscar only by correspondence. He did, however, sign himself to me as " your friend " so his inclusion under the title of this book is, I think, justified.

By an odd coincidence Wilde's son Cyril was at Radley during my last year there, while my correspondence with his father was going on. No one except the Warden knew that Cyril Holland was Cyril Wilde: the Warden kept the secret. I remember Holland, a dark-haired, rather plump, rather sallow little boy; I do not remember ever having spoken to him. He was, as is generally known, killed in the first World War.

It is only within the last few years that I have

moved, on occasion, in what might be called " the Wilde circle " of today, that is, in the company of those who are specialists in Wilde, who write about him and collect his letters and manuscripts and first editions. It is emphatically not a homosexual circle; its members are attracted to Wilde—absorbed by him, I might say of some of them—because of his personality and his writings, not because of any sympathy with his sexual vocation. I have been admitted to their company because Wilde wrote letters to me. When appearing among these enthusiasts, these Oscar experts, I feel instantly and completely stripped of all my reasons of being and states of being except the one reason and the one state, on these occasions splendidly sole, of my association with Wilde. I am introduced as " the Radley boy who wrote letters to Oscar ". I don't at all mind this obliteration of any other aspects that I may have. Indeed, I like it, it gives me a sense of designated security and repose. Sometimes it makes me feel as though I had been given a good part in a good play.

Five unknown letters of Wilde have lately come into my possession since the death of my old and admired friend, that fine fanatic, George Ives. Their special interest is in their difference from other letters of Wilde because of their reflection of this particular correspondent's character which was so unlike his own. Wilde had known

Ives for a long time, he knew his character. He did not know me; he imagined me. He could be more like himself in writing to a stranger over whom his imagination could have free play than he could be to a known friend with whom he was not wholly in sympathy. George Ives had little æsthetic sense, he was completely indifferent to his surroundings and to what he ate and drank. He was not, when Wilde lived, so much of a recluse as he became in later years, and his discipleship of Walt Whitman gave him the impulse to mix with " low-life " strangers. These facts account for his strangely inappropriate suggestion that Wilde and he should meet " where cochers de fiacre resort ". His lack of humour is also seen in this suggestion which was, I am sure, seriously made. Another life-long characteristic of his, fanaticism, may be read between the lines of these letters by those who knew him. Already, at the turn of the century, he was a dedicated crusader against the anti-homosexual provisions of the Criminal Law Amendment Act to which one of these letters refers.

At that time, in his early thirties, Ives had started work on his *History of Penal Methods*, a classic of its kind that took up nearly half of his long life. Comprehensive though it is, it was inspired solely by the passionate urgency of his wish to help to abolish a law that he thought barbarously cruel and unjust. Oscar Wilde, to him, was a martyr. After Wilde's conviction he swore never again to drink any intoxicant, and he kept this vow.

That these two men were well enough acquainted in earlier days to be on Christian name terms is shown by the first letter, undated as Wilde's letters nearly always were; and in this case there is no postmark to date it as it was written at the New Travellers' Club to which it was addressed:

Dear George, I am charmed to see you are at the Albany—I am off to the country till Monday. I have said I am going to Cambridge to see you—but I am really going to see the young Domitian, who has taken to poetry!

Next week let us meet. Yrs Oscar.

Those who know *The Importance of Being Earnest* will remember " Bunbury " and " Bunburying ". Ives was the " Bunbury " on that occasion.

The next letter is of March, 1898, and was written from the Hotel de Nice, Rue des Beaux-Arts, Paris, where Wilde lived before he moved to the Hotel d'Alsace in the same street.

My Dear George, Thanks so much for your letter: your charming friend came to see me one morning at the Hotel—and was most delightful—I hope to see him again in a few days—He seems quite fascinated by Paris.

Thanks so much for ordering my book—it is now in its Fifth Edition—Smithers has put a flaming advertisement into the Athenæum—Headed

" 3000 copies sold in three weeks "—

When I read it I feel like Lipton's tea—!

Yes: I have no doubt we shall win—but the road is long, and red with monstrous martyrdoms—

Nothing but the repeal of the Criminal Law Amendment Act would do any good. That is the essential. It is not so much public opinion, as public officials that need educating.

ever yrs   Oscar.

The book referred to is *The Ballad of Reading Gaol*, then just published by Leonard Smithers.

The third letter was written nearly two years later from the Hotel d'Alsace.

Thank you very much for the book—it's powerfully written—of course it lacks style—but between Truth and Style there is always a désaccord—unless one is a poet.

The ideas in the book are excellent—but the mode of presentation lacks charm—The book stimulates but does not win one—

But I am glad to have it.

I know you *intended* to put yr address in yr telegram—but the habit—the bad habit of secretiveness made you omit it.

What a warning!

I have no doubt your little eating house—where the cochers de fiacre go—is delightful to you—but really George, it is hardly the place to invite others to—you should keep it as a private luxury—a cheap haven of unrest—

When you come again to Paris I hope you will breakfast with *me*—I know lots of nice, quiet, seemly places—where we can talk—rien n'est sacré a un cocher de fiacre—Besides, they are revolting personally.

Bosie is over here—with his brother—they are in deep mourning and the highest spirits—the English are like that—

I am delighted you are interested in the cover of yr book—I always *began* with the cover—

Lord Alfred Douglas (" Bosie ") and his elder brother were no doubt in mourning for their father, the Marquess of Queensberry who brought about Wilde's downfall. His death would account for the high spirits of his two sons, both of whom detested him, as he them. The elder had once come to blows with him in Bond Street, and the younger had egged Wilde on to prosecute him for criminal libel, hoping to see his father sent to prison. I do not know the name of the book referred to in this letter, but it was evidently the kind of serious, propagandist book that would have appealed to George Ives

The next letter was written in September, 1900.

My Dear George, I am very glad your book has been received well—I hope it will give you the position you deserve—

I will be charmed to see you in Paris—but you must come to proper, seemly restaurants—not go to dreadful cabarets where cochers de fiacre resort—I hope you will never lose the sense of style in life—it keeps the barbarians away.

I know you are not rich*—but I wonder could you lend me £10 till October 1st: I get my small income thro' Robbie Ross on the first of each month—and could ask him to pay you back direct. I am in great worry and annoyance over money—the price of my rooms has been doubled owing to the Exhibition—and my landlord presses me.

If you can do this, would you mind sending notes in a registered letter—cheques take ages to cash. Yrs Oscar.

Ives sent the money at once, for the letter that follows is postmarked three days later.

Many thanks—it is most kind of you.

I hope you will come over soon—and not alone: but don't conceal your charming friends—you usually hide them from me.

Your book that you promised me has never arrived—do let me have a copy.

Paris has gone back to summer weather—and

* Ives had a thousand a year, so, if not "rich", was certainly well off in those days.

the problem of how to dress is acute. One never knows what the day is going to be like.

What a charming book Edward Carpenter's—" Civilization, Cause and Cure " is—it is most suggestive. I constantly read it.

Ever, with my thanks, Yours Oscar.

" Your book ", referred to in these last two letters, must have been a much earlier and slighter one of Ives' than the *History of Penal Methods*. In the last letter the two sentences about the weather are noteworthy because they have no Oscarian flavour. Throughout the letter that flavour is weak. It was rarely indeed that Wilde made a commonplace observation in commonplace language. When he wrote that about the Paris weather he must have been feeling most exceptionally dull and depressed. It was not long before his death, which his closest friend, Robert Ross, knew to be " a release ".

Ross was with him when he died and wrote to me a few weeks later that " Though the circumstances of his death were very painful in many ways he did not actually suffer during the last two days of his life, being quite unconcious. . . . The end was quite unexpected, although he had been ill for some weeks. . . . It was in many ways for the best. He was very unhappy and would have become more unhappy as time went on. In most cases this is said merely as a matter of form and a convention of comfort but in this particular instance it really can be said with perfect truth."

He was unhappy not so much because he was poor, although he often complained of his poverty. Incurably extravagant, he would have complained of that unless he had been really rich. As an exile in Paris he was adequately, though not lavishly provided for. What made him unhappy was that Society's punishment of him did not end with his imprisonment. After his "disgrace", only a very few were left from the crowd of companions and disciples and sycophants of his triumphant days. He had tried living with Alfred Douglas; an experiment that saddeningly failed, and no wonder.

Afterwards, in Paris, he was the object of frequent slights and affronts from people who a few years earlier had been boastful of their acquaintanceship with him. He felt such treatment keenly. Oscar Browning told me of an occasion on which he passed Wilde in a Paris street, a year or so after his release. The " O.B." was driving in a cab, Wilde was walking in the opposite direction, and their eyes met. For that moment the recognition happened to be on Wilde's side only, and he concluded that this former acquaintance of his was another one of the many who now chose deliberately to " cut " him. " When I had passed him," said O.B., " I realized who he was: and then it was too late. The sudden pain in his eyes was unforgettable." In this case the slight was not intentional, but in scores of others it was premeditated. When I related this incident to a very intimate and always loyal friend of Wilde, he shrugged his shoulders and observed shortly that that was the kind of thing that was perpetually happening.

Another cause of the unhappiness of those last years was inability to work. It is known that *The Ballad of Reading Gaol* and *De Profundis* were composed almost entirely in prison. When he was free, he found he could write nothing. He could have got money, of course, by lending himself to journalistic sensation-mongering. Offers were received from representatives of the " yellow " Press, baited by considerable sums, for articles from Wilde on " A Day of my Life in Prison ", " Reminiscences of my Trial ", and the like. One answer of his is well-known. " I cannot understand," he said, " how such a proposal can be made to any gentleman."

During the last five years of his life Oscar Wilde was a ruined man, flung from eminence into obloquy. Today his rare distinction as a figure in literary history has never been more clearly seen.

FRANK HARRIS

IT was Aleister Crowley who, in New York in the autumn of 1915, introduced me to Frank Harris. During the next three or four years I was in the United States and saw Harris often. When he was living in Nice during the 'twenties I used to see him whenever I was in the south of France up to his death in 1931. When he gave me copies of his books he inscribed them " to my friend " or " from his friend ", but we were friends in the looser, the more superficial sense. I wonder if anyone ever was in real friendship with Frank Harris? I doubt it. He was a wonder, but he was not distinguished for the qualities that provoke real friendship.

Few would deny that he was more important as a person than as a writer. No one who knew him can forget him. His survival will depend, I think, more surely upon what is written about him than upon what he wrote; upon Hugh Kingsmill's biography, upon the same writer's novel *The Will to Love*, of which Harris is the hero or villain, and upon other shorter accounts of him that have been given. Wilde's remark, " I have put my genius into my life, only my talent into my work ", could have been made with much greater truth by Frank Harris.

Yet it would hardly be just to say that as

a writer he achieved nothing. Some Shakespearian scholars will probably continue to feel regard for his writings on Shakespeare, which Max Beerbohm declared that he valued more highly than those of the professors; because of their originality and unprofessorial character, no doubt. In his short stories Harris shows a story-teller's gift; he has vigour, grip, and sense of technique, but no sense of character to fructify his sense of action. Occasionally he " brought it off ", as by a lucky fluke, and it should be remembered that George Meredith said of *Montes the Matador:* " If there is a hand in England that can do better, I do not know of it." But, in general, Harris lacks any distinction, is headlong and careless, with the faults of a slipshod journalism. *My Life and Loves,* though often very readable when he is talking about the men and women of his time and not about his love-affairs—which he makes monotonous and unreal—is from any critical standpoint almost worthless. With the best will in the world not many can feel convinced that, whatever the occasional interest of his writing, Harris was really a writer. His nature did not mean him to be one. To express himself he needed the stimulus of company, food, and wine. When he wrote, he rarely if ever wrote disinterestedly, but with an eye to the main chance and in the competitive spirit. " I can do better than Kipling! " " I can beat Maupassant! " How often have I heard him say things like that.

Harris, like Aleister Crowley, was vain; but Crowley could never have thought of himself as in that kind of competition with anyone. He would not have aimed at " beating " anyone, I think, except at his favourite game of chess: certainly not at writing. He was proud as well as vain. He was more like Harris in another respect. Both of them blundered because of incapacity to understand normal human characteristics. Harris could not succeed for long as a financier because he did not know men; and he could not make a real success as a writer for the same reason. Bernard Shaw wrote to me in 1927: " It is useless to try to find a publisher for F.H. His attempt to smooth the way by conciliating his enemies ended so disastrously that no publisher will venture on purely business grounds. He must wait until some admiring young publisher volunteers." His *Contemporary Portraits* and his biographies of Wilde and Shaw fail, as his fiction fails, because he cannot see people as they are. It was an odd experience, reading the " contemporary portrait " that he did of me and finding myself an unreal stranger, a character of Harris fiction.

He was born a year after Oscar Wilde and a year before Bernard Shaw. That Wilde enjoyed his company is evident from some of Wilde's published letters. Harris may or may not— accounts are variable—have treated Wilde shabbily over the play in which they collaborated, *Mr. and Mrs. Daventry*. However that may be, he was certainly often a good friend, within his limitations, to Wilde. He did not turn his back on him after the débacle. One can indeed hardly imagine Frank Harris, always a rebel against all conventional morality, doing that. " I don't mind what they do," he told me once when we were talking about " Uranians ", " so long as they don't try to do it to me." Max Beerbohm's cartoon of Harris and Shakespeare— " Perhaps if Shakespeare had asked me "— comes to mind in this connection. It was to be expected that Harris would be not only as friendly and as companionable to Wilde after " the fall " as he always had been, but more so. He was; and, to some extent at least, he helped him. Before the trial, Harris knew very well what the half-crazy, spoiled-darling egotism of Alfred Douglas meant for Oscar, and what worse harm it was likely to do him. He did his best to dissuade Wilde from the disastrous act, urged by Douglas with such hysterical vehemence, of prosecuting " the Scarlet Marquess " for libel. " Ah! Ancient Pistol! " Douglas once called out derisively, passing Harris in the Café Royal. " Well roared, Bottom! " was Harris's instant retort.

I never heard Harris speak of Douglas without contempt or of Wilde without admiration. Disparagement of Bernard Shaw was, I soon found, a habit of his; he was envious of Shaw's fame and wealth. His having helped Shaw considerably by giving him work on the *Saturday Review* when he was editor of that paper seemed to make his envy the more bitter. Shaw never forgot what Harris had done for him, he was always kind to Harris, always did what he could for him, but that made no difference. Harris was all the more envious because he thought himself a greater writer than Shaw. He was convinced that his own play, *Joan la Romée*, was much superior to Shaw's *Saint Joan*. Whereas even the police official who came to visit me after Harris had sent me his banned *Life and Loves* through the mails could see that *Joan la Romée* was "just rather a nice little piece for school-kiddies, no harm in it—nothing much at all". But when Harris declared, in his terrific voice, "Of curse (as he pronounced "course") I shall outlive Shaw, of curse I shall!", though the context of the conversation showed that he meant "physically outlive", I knew that he was thinking that he was equally certain to outlive Shaw as a writer.

Shaw's asceticism was one of his favourite subjects for ridicule. I should like to have heard him expressing the disgust and derision that he told me he did express when Shaw told him that he was in his late twenties when he first had a woman. "And he seemed to think that was *normal!* No blood, the man never had any blood!" Shaw came to see him in the nineteen-twenties at Nice, and talked jestingly of "Your fierce moustache, Frank—your thick black hair, your manly voice—your bandit's face—why, no young woman would dare come near you! But think of the advantages of *my* senile appearance. No young woman could be afraid of *me*. They come and sit on my knee, Frank—without a moment's hesitation—think of that, Frank, think of that! You should dye your hair white "— and so on.

How far this report by Harris of what Shaw said is to be trusted is of course uncertain. But it was characteristic of Harris in his relation to Shaw that he should have repeated those imagined or real or touched-up pleasantries as he did, with such hostility and venomous scorn.

What a fellow he was, though, for all that! Remembering him, I feel it is mean of me to pick out his faults and failings. What a fellow, with his short thick-set body, his large head with its abnormally large nose and ears, his young-looking hair and moustache—if they were dyed they were very cleverly dyed—his full, gross lips and his booming voice which Thomas Hardy described as " the gruffest voice I ever heard." I shouldn't have called it " gruff "; it was not unmusical; it had an attractive timbre, a rich, voluptuous resonance, a not unpleasing though sometimes rather comical imitation of aristocratic accent; it was indeed a potent, memorable voice, and it enhanced the brilliant impressiveness of his talk, giving it what was almost a hypnotic effect. The general and special effects of his spoken words never appeared in his writings. He was the best talker I have known. Whatever his subject, he talked superbly, with natural eloquence. There were no " thin places "; he was never slack or tedious. His luncheon parties in New York and Nice lasted from about two to six with never a dull moment. What he said was always as characteristic as the way he said it. He was often extremely bawdy. The most characteristic flings of his wit and humour are, even today, unprintable. At the same time, and not inconsistently, he had a real feeling for poetry. I remember the ecstasy with which he repeated " Speak silence with thy glimmering eyes, And wash the dusk with silver ": " Dateless oblivion and divine repose ": " Thou hast led me like a heathen sacrifice, With music and with fatal yoke of flowers, To my eternal ruin ". Another quotation had a comic effect—I feel sure unintentionally comic—when he wrote it, as he often did, on the fly-leaf of a presentation copy of a volume of his *Life and Loves:* " But something ere the end, Some deed of noble note may yet be done." His *viva voce* quotations were never so ludicrously irrelevant: and, entertaining his guests, he quoted little, used his own words instead, and was right to do that.

Those luncheon parties! Harris habitually used a stomach-pump so that he could eat more. He was not ashamed but rather proud of that daily habit. Or so I gathered from his insistence on showing me the object in question. He kept his guests at his luncheon table for at least twice as long as is usual, and once at Nice when some of the guests were ladies whom I hardly knew, I found that embarrassing. I resorted to a device that may prove useful to anyone in the same difficulty. The discussion over coffee and liqueurs seemed likely to go on for another half hour or more. I forget the subject, but not the inspiration that made me ejaculate eagerly: " Ah! I've just been reading something in the *Matin* that seemed to clear up that very point. I left the paper in the lobby, may I go and get it? " I returned after a search that was vain but must have seemed thorough. It is curious how, even in the freest of companies, certain conventions will linger.

In his talk Harris sometimes showed an insight that was proved later to have been remarkably true. In January 1918, he gave me an almost exact forecast of the future events of the war— the German " push " in the spring, its temporary success followed first by the counter-success of the Allies, then by their victory, and then by " armistice in the autumn and peace before Christmas." Here was the same startling power of prediction of which Shaw has given an example in one of his Prefaces, relating how Harris told Wilde in exact detail what would happen to him if he sued Lord Queensberry.

Harris could, by a kind of magic, tell the truth before it happened, though he was as a general rule a terrific liar. He may very often, because of his intense subjectivity, have not known he was lying. He has none the less a good claim to the title of the most unscrupulous and richly inventive liar of his century. Nothing that he said or wrote about himself or about anyone else can be believed unless it is firmly corroborated. Of his origins and early life—and of his later life, too—he gave widely varying accounts. It is fairly safe to say that he was part-Irish and part-Welsh. Born in Ireland, the son of a seafaring man, he went to America in his youth to seek his fortune, roughed it there, and later on was a financial and journalistic adventurer in England and in America, finally retiring to Nice. These are the broad outlines of a life that is full of doubtful detail. I wish I could clear up some of those doubts. I wish I could be sure that it was true, that retort he told me he made when, during proceedings taken against him for libel, he was warned that he was dangerously near contempt of court. "No words of mine," he boomed back, "can express one hundredth part of the contempt in which I hold this court!" But did that happen?

Frank Harris could no more be trusted with money than he could be with the truth. He never swindled me nor attempted to—indeed he paid me generously for such contributions as I made to the magazine, *Pearson's*, that he was editing in New York and he frequently entertained me with lavish hospitality both in New

York and in Nice—but he swindled as often as
he could those whom he regarded as suitable
subjects. He was ruthlessly unscrupulous and
lived by being so. He was a thorough-paced
blackguard and the best of good companions,
flagrantly dishonest, shamelessly dishonourable,
but, like Falstaff, a veritable strong water of life,
rousing and reviving everyone who tasted him.
I remember him as I remember certain rare old
brandies. He had the same kind of richness and
power. He was blood-brother to Falstaff in his
roguery, his knavish tricks, his thieving, his lying,
his love of drink, his lechery—and in his conquer-
ing vigour, his eloquence and power of invective,
his swiftness and ease and shrewdness of stroke,
his generosity, the fascination of his whole state
of being. " I could have better spared a
better man."

He was sixty-three when I first met him, and
I continued, with unflagging delight, to know
him until he died at seventy-six. Except during
the last of those thirteen years he showed little
sign of declining mental or physical power. He
did not " outlive Shaw ", he died nearly twenty
years before him. But if will to live could have
done it, he certainly would have lived till well
past ninety. He was a life-lover if ever there
was one.

It was not long before his death that he drew
my attention to one sign of his old age. That

was a pathetic occasion; it was the only occasion when I saw Frank Harris in a pathetic light. We were walking along the Promenade des Anglais at Nice. For some minutes he had been unwontedly silent and absent, and then he told me that he was now completely impotent. With surprising suddenness he had, only the other day, found himself in that condition, to his consternation and horror. " It's got the *mind*, too," he said sadly. " You see those girls—going bathing. They mean nothing to me—absolutely nothing." I said a sympathetic word or two and turned to give him a sympathetic look. His eyes were filled with tears. I remembered that at our first meeting he had boasted to me that at sixty-three he was as good a lover as ever. " Never a flash-in-the-pan! " That may have been one of his lies, or half-lies; but there is no doubt that on this occasion at Nice he was telling the tragic truth.

His sense of wine had been dulled some years before. When he was my guest at a luncheon party near Nice I gave him first a local white wine that I knew he particularly liked and then a Montrachet, a miracle of delicate floweriness. I asked him how he thought they set against each other. " Exactly the same! " he shouted. " They taste to me exactly the same! " On the journey back he fell sound asleep. I sat in the car behind him and noted the old scoundrel's nodding head with what was almost affection. Memories of him came gratefully back to me

36

over the past years—one memory in particular of an afternoon when we were lunching in the garden of some little hotel in the mountains above Nice. " What is the difference," he asked me, " between bobbed and shingled hair ? " I told him that shingled hair looked like a boy's, behind.

" A boy's behind ? " he said, and I never heard even his voice resound so richly and so hugely as it did with those words. The Alpes Maritimes echoed and re-echoed to that great shout. " *A boy's behind!* How much longer am I to sit here and listen to your obscene conversation ? I've never seen a boy's behind. I've never *wished* to see a boy's behind! Any *other* simile ! A boy's—" Then, from sheer joy, he kicked a little dog who happened to be within reach, kicked it with vigour.

The faces of the British tourists at the table next to ours suffered change while he was speaking. They were solid, respectable, bourgeois tourists, and Harris thoroughly enjoyed violating them.

Full measure—profuse, wasteful, inordinate— of the spirit of life, good spirit and bad spirit, had been poured into this man. An arch-egoist with a powerful, undisciplined brain, both coarse and fine, with no moral sense of any sort, he was born to make a big splash and to half-drown himself in it. He was a man of violent projections, brutal, gross, sentimental and yet poetic; outrageous in a score of ways, a buccaneering, bully-boy interloper into the literary world, a pirate hoisting up his own rebellious, defiant flag, his hand against every man's and every man's hand against him; but as a person, as a talker, he was surely a man of genius. He was the most remarkable literary blackguard of almost any century.

ALEISTER CROWLEY

So much has been written about Aleister Crowley since his death that my first thought before writing about him is of what should be left out rather than of what should be put in. In addition to several magazine articles, five books have been published lately: Crowley's official Life, *The Great Beast*, by John Symonds, in which Crowley appears in what many of his disciples feel to be an unjustifiably evil and lurid light: Charles Cammell's shorter account of him as Poet and Mage, strongly appreciative for the most part, sometimes eulogistic, but not a " whitewash ": three other books in which he figures, Clifford Bax's *Some I Knew Well*, with its friendly and amusing sketch of Crowley, Arthur Calder Marshall's *The Magic of My Youth*, and Denis Clark's *Sword Fish and Stromboli*.

Crowley was important in my life, from 1907 or 1908 until he died at the end of 1947. From 1915 to 1919, in America, I got to know him well, better still during the seven years before the second war, and best of all during the five or six years before his death. Unlike most others who have written of him I was not a " disciple ". We hardly ever discussed magic. Nor did we talk much about sex. These two subjects are of course those most closely associated with Aleister

Crowley: indeed one might say that there is no
other association with him in the public mind,
and that his fame, or infamy, rests on those two
supports of sex and magic alone, on those two
unrivalled magnetic pillars that can always draw
so many with such power.

Early in the second war the unhappy
William Joyce broadcast a suggestion that,
as our Intercession Services didn't seem to be
doing much good, Crowley should be invited to
celebrate a Black Mass in Westminster Abbey.
This was about the time when Crowley was
gravely ill at Torquay and had written to me that
the reporters were lurking in the rose-bushes of
the garden of his hotel, " waiting to hear of my
death ". I disbelieved him then, thinking that
both he and Joyce exaggerated his publicity
value, but after the splash in the newspapers that
followed his actual death and his funeral I felt
that he might well have been speaking the truth.
Nearly all the newspaper notices were front-page
and they nearly all of them struck the same note:
" Crowley Dies "—" ' Wickedest Man in
Britain ' "—" World's Worst Man "—" ' Black
Magic ' Farewell "—" Cremating ' Great
Beast ' ", and the like. " Crowley's Doctor
Dies " was another headline. He died within a
day of Crowley and the suggestion was of course
made that a curse had been put on him.

After Crowley's unusual funeral the press
notices were still more excitable than they had
been after his death and there were more of them

and longer ones. The day before the funeral, which I spent at the Hastings hotel where he died, the telephone rang frequently for answers to enquiries about the impending ceremony and the names of those who were to attend it. This became tiresome, particularly as there was so much that had to be done. I lost patience with one reporter, refused with some acerbity to give any names, and observed that this was " a private affair ".

The ceremony at Brighton, in the undenominational chapel of the Crematorium, can well be described as peculiar and was far from private. On one side were the mourners—most of the women well dressed enough for their clothes to receive detailed mention in the newspaper accounts—and on the other side were the reporters. Facing this sharply divided congregation I obeyed Crowley's written instructions by reading his *Hymn of Pan*, then extracts from *The Book of the Law* which he believed to have been dictated to him by a supernatural being, then Collects from the Gnostic Mass. The *Hymn of Pan* was occasionally interrupted by ecstatic cries of " Io Pan ! " from devotees, and the words with which Crowley began and ended his letters— " Do what thou wilt shall be the whole of the Law " and " Love is the Law, Love under Will " —were interspersed throughout the reading with religious fervour. Some of the mourners grew more and more emotional as the reading went on, while the reporters looked more and more

comically bewildered, or nonplussed. Carna-
tions were thrown by a beautiful girl upon the
coffin as it slid downwards. When the Brighton
Corporation next met they resolved that no such
pagan and blasphemous ceremony—on conse-
crated ground, too!—should ever again be
permitted within their jurisdiction. " Dese-
crated by Black Magic " was one of the headlines
then. There has certainly never been a funeral
like Crowley's in England, not a public one at
any rate. No sooner were we out of the chapel
than the reporters advanced upon us for information. " Better take care what you write! " my
co-literary executor warned one of them.
" Crowley will get at you from wherever he is! "
What a day! In the Crowley circle, as in the
Wilde circle, I have one aspect only: that of
" the man who read the *Hymn of Pan* at the
Beast's Funeral."

There was a dinner at an Indian restaurant to
commemorate the first anniversary of Crowley's
death. The Press got hold of that and most of
us who were known to be connected with the
Master were rung up during the afternoon.
Before the dinner some animosity was shown
towards the reporters by disciples who felt that
Crowley had been disrespectfully treated by the
newspapers in the accounts of his death and
funeral. Public interest in him was evidently
thought to be still alive later on when his Will
was proved (at eighteen pounds). I had then
left London, but one reporter managed to get

my telephone number in the country and we had a conversation of about twenty minutes that must have cost the newspaper something, as it was not during the cheaper telephone hours. I was moved to go all out for Crowley on that occasion. In reply to the question " What was Crowley's purpose in life? " I said " The regeneration of the world," and gave the further information that Crowley's Temples were scattered all the world over, " even behind the Iron Curtain," and that his ashes now sanctified the High Altar of the chief Temple in the United States. These statements cannot perhaps be proved to be wholly true, but they are by no means wholly false. " He must have been an extraordinary man," said the reporter, and he did not seem to say it ironically. " He *is* an extraordinary man," I replied.

And so he is, or was. I leave out of count his magical powers of which I know nothing. The pity is that his nose was too small; otherwise he would, I believe, have been indisputably a great man, both as a writer and as a religious leader. Vanity was his handicap. He was too sure of his genius to criticize or to revise adequately his own work. He thought that everything he wrote must be good. Impatient to see his books printed and wishing to have them set up and bound in his own lavish way, he rarely tried to find a publisher, so their circulation was strictly limited. The

D

43

books of his that were published, such as *The Diary of a Drug Fiend* and *Moon Child*, were perhaps his worst. But all his books had by no means inconsiderable faults. His poetry could be very bad as well as very good. He could write mere imitative pieces, he could write superbly, with an exultant vigour entirely his own, but he never seemed to know whether he was doing the one or the other. He could also write masterly lampoons in verse. *To a Slim Gilt Soul*, his lampoon on Alfred Douglas— " Giton and Judas and Tartuffe " he calls him— is perhaps the best of these. It is published in *Oscar Wilde and the Black Douglas*. Of his graver vein in verse an example, a timely one, is " Kill off mankind, And give the earth a chance; Nature may find In her inheritance Some seedlings of a race Less infinitely base." His happy and high-spirited lines " O for a lily-white goat, Crisp as a thicket of thorns, With a collar of gold for its throat, And a scarlet bow for its horns " are equally Crowleian; and characteristic of his parody vein is " O English girl, half baby and half bitch! "

An anthology should be made of Crowley's poems, for those that really are poems, his best ones, among which I would doubt if those published in *The Oxford Book of Mystical Verse* should be included, would fill a fair-sized volume. The anthology, *Olla*, that he made himself and had printed shortly before his death, was planned so as to represent the varieties of his verse-writing: there are good poems in it—notably two that he wrote at the end of his life—but there are many too many inferior poems as well. Crowley wouldn't take my advice about *Olla*. He always thought I failed to appreciate him as a poet. After reading a book of mine in which I laid perhaps too much stress upon his remarkable gifts for cooking, he wrote these lines on the fly-leaf: " On Crowley the Immortals ironically look, He sought fame as a poet and he found it as a cook."

Well, I could not understand most of his mystical poetry, though I could respond to some of it—to such lines (I quote from memory) as:

> The Universe I measured with my rod,
> The blacks were even with the whites.
> Satan dropped down as uprose God,
> Whores danced and played with anchorites.
> So in my Book the even matched the odd.
> No word therein I wrote,
> But signed it with the Sigil of the Goat.

On the other hand, I could fully appreciate his cooking and his taste in wine and old brandy. I can never forget that 1912 Martinez, perfectly decanted and at a perfect temperature, that he had for me after a dinner to celebrate my birthday; and I have not enjoyed any meals more than those that Crowley has cooked. Curry was, at Crowley's, the *specialité de la maison*: those curries were astounding. They were rather too moving for me, though I ate them with joy for their very excessiveness. Crowley cooked steak with consummate skill and with an ardour that did not burn with that same excess of heat, so, although his curries won the wider fame, his steaks gave the larger sum of pleasure. Those steaks, with a bottle of Richebourg or Corton —Burgundy and port were his favourite wines— are what I remember most gratefully. But Crowley could touch no food that he did not adorn.

For all that, no cooking, however strong or subtle, leaves footprints on the sands of time. Crowley's future reputation must of course depend mainly upon his writings. His book on the Tarot, produced as the Anthology was near the end of his life, was, he felt, one of the most important of these; and on that massive volume I am not qualified to express an opinion. Some of the pictures of the Tarot cards by Frieda Harris are of a terrifying originality and nearly all of them are enthralling. The originals, of which there were exhibitions in Oxford and London, are naturally still more impressive. This Tarot book is sumptuously produced; no wonder it cost ten guineas. Crowley told me that he had made fifteen hundred pounds from it in three months. " Now you see," he then said, " how idiotic it is to have a publisher." I pointed out that the very considerable cost of producing the book should be put to the debit account. Crowley looked surprised. " Oh, of course," he said, " if the author is fool enough to pay for the printing and binding—" I might have reminded him that that was what in the old days he had always been fool enough to do. Then he was a rich man, but as soon as he had spent all his money—his extravagance in many directions was fantastic—his devotees paid the expenses of his books, and whatever proceeds there were, were his.

It was characteristic of Crowley that he took this money as his rightful due. He did quite honestly, and, when you think of it, not unnaturally feel that it was as much a matter of course for others to pay for the production of his magical books, or indeed of any of his books, as it had been for him himself to pay when he had the money. If people who had money, now that he had not, paid also for his personal upkeep, thus enabling him to " accomplish the great work," that was only to be expected, too. His attitude had nothing in common with that of the vulgar exploiting charlatan. It may be called naïve, and so in a sense it was, but it seemed to him entirely natural and right. And, after all, he had a great deal to give that no one else had to the disciples who contributed to the support of his cause and himself.

I was never a contributor, but he had a great deal to give me, and gave it none the less for that. In conversation he gave richly. What a lot of pleasure I have had from his talk during all the periods of my friendship with him; except during the last month or so of his life when he was ill and under the now deadening influence of his drugs. " I am sorry you have wasted your time in visiting a log," were the last words he said to me, very soon before he died. He had come to the end; his wit, so much his own, and his wakeful, surprising intelligence with its various sudden glancing thrusts, had failed him. But in his youth and in his prime, and long after, he was memorable for his peculiar dynamics of attraction and fascination. I do not believe that he will be forgotten. What has been written about him will materially help to impress him upon posterity, but, as Doctor Johnson would have survived without Boswell, so would Crowley survive without contemporary biographers. He would not like this comparison, for he detested Doctor Johnson and said that he represented all that was worst in the English character. What would Doctor Johnson have said of him?

As to Crowley's morals, there is no doubt truth in the accusations of unscrupulousness and even of what most people would consider wickedness that have been so freely brought against him. Many of these charges are entirely baseless, but of a few there is proof. None the less, he had his own integrity. When he was living in Paris in the 'twenties he was offered a substantial sum of money to cast horoscopes for a girl and a man with indications that the two were exceptionally well suited to each other and destined to a happy marriage. This was suggested by a *sale individu* who would have had a considerable commission if the marriage had happened: the girl was rich. Crowley, at that time particularly hard up, refused. The individual then told him that he could and would prevent the renewal of his visa if he did not cast the horoscopes. Crowley, knowing that this was so, knowing the man's back-stairs pull with the authorities concerned, still refused, with the result that he had in due course to leave Paris under the obloquy of having been kicked out.

His integrity appeared also in the last years of his life when he was in need of a trained nurse. A friend suggested that he should have one but he told her he hadn't money enough. "But," she reminded him, "there's nearly five hundred pounds in that strong box."

"That's not for my personal use," he replied. "It's money from America, earmarked for the Order." His friend persuaded him, but with some difficulty, that the health of himself as head of the Order was one of its more important purposes, and he gave way. If it had not been for this attested incident, I might have found more difficulty than I did as executor in persuading the Official Receiver that the cash in Crowley's possession at his death—then about four hundred and fifty pounds—was money entrusted to him for specific purposes, religious purposes, not his own money, and therefore not liable for distribution among his creditors, but due to be returned (as it was) to its giver in America.

As Crowley has the reputation of having been always utterly unscrupulous about money, any qualification that there is of his unscrupulousness should not be omitted. To me there seemed a good deal that was admirable and attractive as well as reprehensible about his behaviour to money. The inheritor in his youth of a considerable fortune, he spent it all on those richly coloured, imaginative manias that can beggar a man more quickly than any mere luxuries. Crowley threw every one of his singular, passionate intensities into spending all that he had. He treated his fortune as a toy. If you fit out mountaineering expeditions and are continually printing sumptuous private editions of your poems and plays and magical works, and buying places in Scotland, and living everywhere like a prince and entertaining like a Maharajah, even a large fortune won't last very long. But what *panache*, what *élan* and *brio* while it does last! Extravagance can be simply silly, but in Crowley's extravagance there was imagination and even a sort of sublime faith. The most egregiously inappropriate epithet ever applied to him is " sordid ". " Surely the most sordid and shabby of charlatans " is what one reviewer wrote of him. Of course a man can live richly and yet be shabby and sordid in himself, but that was not so with Crowley.

I didn't know him when he had all those thousands, I knew him after they had all gone, but he always gave the impression of being carelessly rich, he always managed that somehow. Except once, some time in the 'thirties, when I found him living in Paddington Green in some frightful lodging. I never knew how that happened. Very likely it wasn't because of poverty but for some entirely different reason. He spent a great deal of money for his magic, for his religion; he may have been living in Paddington Green for the sake of his religion. His craziest actions were based on the coldest logic. Even at that time he gave only a momentary impression of poverty. Almost at once his background didn't exist. There was incense burning, I remember; of course that may have helped. The Paddington Green interlude didn't last long; very soon it was Piccadilly and Jermyn Street again. I always felt that Aleister was the right sort of man to have money; too many people who have it are the wrong sort.

No doubt he could give the impression of ostentation, of " charlatan " ostentation, not only by the *grand seigneur* air that he sometimes adopted, but by his vagaries of dress, his breeches with eighteenth-century silver buckles, his enormous green scarf, his Chinese beard, and heavy seal with Tarot devices. He has been compared with William Beckford, but " ostentation " is a term that much better suits Beckford, who was always making a show with his money, depended on it and on his social position, exploited his oddity and conceit, and had no real power in himself. He could not have borne to live at all humbly. Crowley, on the other hand, although he had money enough in his last years to live as expensively as he nearly always had, lived instead at an unpretentious boarding-house at Hastings because he liked the proprietor and his wife, both of whom also liked him. He was well looked after there, the place suited him, but it was certainly not a place with which an ostentatious man would have been contented. His going to live there was arranged at my suggestion by my son who was then living at Hastings and who was very soon writing to me of Crowley's " caressing charm " and " careless wit ". But my son, like many others, influenced by Crowley's reputation as something monstrous and inhuman, thought him " a very dangerous man ", though he appreciated his humour and his mind and, above all, his strangeness, so they got on well together. To some people he was certainly dangerous, even fatal. But I doubt very much if he ever " disintegrated " anyone's " personality " unless that personality was well on the way towards disintegration.

Whatever Crowley's morals or lack of them, I should remember with the same deep gratification that he told me, towards the end of his life, that I was his greatest friend. I was certainly closer to him then than I had been before; partly because I had come to know him more intimately and partly because there was then, to me at least, an affecting pathos about him, a pathos of which he may have been sometimes conscious, though he never played for pity. I had always felt that there was something of pathos about him but in his last years this element seemed to me much stronger and he was in consequence lovable as I had not known him to be before. He knew then that he had not done what he wanted to do, that he had done only a part of it: he knew that, during his lifetime at least, he would have infamy rather than fame. When he had been again dangerously ill a year or two before his death he inscribed a book to the man who had devotedly tended him: "To —, who saved my worthless life," and it is likely that in some moods he did think of his life as worthless. His vanity, which had amounted to something at least near megalomania, took backward paces.

Success and recognition in the usual sense would, I think, have weaned him from this vanity which was to some considerable extent his substitute for them. He was a great man *manqué*, and that set him awry. He resorted to a self-advertisement that became more violent as he grew less sure of the power that he had for achieving his end. That end, he had believed, could be gained—and how easily!—by the energies that he knew to be so abundant in himself. Crowley's tragedy was that, as he aged, he came to know it could not. At any rate, though he had materially failed and was pained by that failure, he never resorted to " repentance ". No such disgusting exhibitionism marked his last days as marked those of the really evil Gilles de Raiz, whose vanity staged scenes of confession and " contrition " almost as nauseating as his crimes were. " I am perplexed ", were the only dying words of Crowley.

That he really did believe himself to be by destiny a great religious regenerator, that he had full faith in the religion which he built upon his " Law of Thelema " to bring the world nearer to what he called " Godhead ", I have no doubt. I knew him well enough not to have any, although I was never, as I have said, even a novice in his religion, let alone an initiate. But more than once I have seen him under the sudden stress of his inspiration. He was controlled, I was sure of it then, by something that was in truth religious, that had the quality, the motive force of Oriental religious ecstasy. One such occasion was during the second war. Crowley and I had been lunching with Lady Aberconway and had gone back with her to his rooms in Jermyn Street where he read aloud to us from an enormous Magical Book which he supported on his knees. What he read was in a strange language, a language unknown. It was of a singular vibrant beauty and power. Christabel Aberconway sat on the floor by his chair with the unwitting grace and ease possible, in such a position, only to a woman of natural-born and fulfilled beauty. Her lovely eyes were large with an emotion that I shared. " What is that language? " she asked. " It is the language of the angels," replied Crowley. Impressed though I was by the exaltation, the irradiation, which he had received and communicated, I could not help reflecting on what an admirable subject the scene would have made for a cartoon by Max Beerbohm. " Aleister Crowley reciting to Lady Aberconway in the Language of the Angels."

At about that same time I tried to get Crowley to tell me what he remembered of his former incarnations. I asked him if it were not a tremendous moment when a former incarnation was first revealed; but Crowley said no, it didn't happen like that, but a fragment of memory would come, generally some insignificant fragment, and other memories would come later, the significant ones appearing imperfectly and obscurely and gradually, often with long intervals between them.

" Reincarnation! " " Language of the Angels! " How easy to ridicule Crowley, to make of him a figure of fun. As easy as to make him out a monster. There were certainly aspects of him that could appear comically. He was in some ways oddly innocent, with the innocence of a Pierrot or a Charlie Chaplin. He could not acquire an adult eye for the main chance or an adult view of the world, of which he knew so little that he was incapable of dealing with it. He blundered time after time because he couldn't learn what the world was like. If he had had any worldly wisdom, or even common sense, he would never have brought that absurd libel action which of course he lost and which made him an undischarged bankrupt for the last twenty years or so of his life.

The same egregious unworldliness appears in him as a writer. He wanted to appeal to the general reader but he never could because he knew nothing about him. Like Robert Browning (whom he much admired), he assumed that he was a specialist. For this reason even if Crowley's works had all been published, and published effectively, it is improbable that they would have had large sales. In his lighter writing there is often this same baulking erudition, there are references and words that most people would find unintelligible and therefore irritating. When I told him so, he said, " But they can always use dictionaries," not seeming to realize at all that if you write only for people who expect to have to use dictionaries when they read you, you are not likely to have many readers. Crowley, however, could no more imagine a reader without reference books at his elbow than he could imagine him without a shirt to his back. He had no sort of flair for what puts the reader off or for what puts him on; he knew none of the practical tricks of the literary trade. In planning with me a " popular " edition of his *Commentary on The Book of the Law* he suggested that a second Commentary, from another hand, should be included.

In his humour, though not in his wit, he was often like a clever schoolboy, and in other ways too. Like many other Englishmen he had in some ways never grown up. He loved to invent and to play ingenious—sometimes maddeningly ingenious—word-games. The same youthful ingenuity would appear when he wrote or spoke sequence after sequence of absurdities so elaborate and so overworked as to become too frequently tedious. He could be terse enough, though, as when he wrote a one-line review in *The Equinox* of a book by a man called Holly: " Holly, Holly, Holly, Lord God Almighty! "

He was terse, too, in a reply that I heard him make to Theodore Dreiser. It was in New York, during the first world war. Dreiser, after protesting earnestly and at length against the dependence of American Letters upon English tradition, asked him, " What have *you* to offer us? " Crowley replied with the single word " Patronage." I still remember Dreiser's rage, it was wonderful. At that time Crowley was experimenting with the drug anhelonium and used to give " anhelonium parties ". I persuaded Dreiser to come to one. He did so with some misgiving. " It will take treble the usual dose to move Dreiser," said Crowley as he prepared it for him. Dreiser, none the less, drank his glass of " the mixture " at one gulp, with determined bravado. Then he felt a little uneasy. He asked Crowley if there was a good doctor in the neighbourhood, " just in case anything goes wrong." " I don't know about a doctor," said Crowley, " but," he added in a tone of genial reassurance, " there's a first-class undertaker on the corner of Thirty-third Street and Sixth Avenue." Dreiser said nothing for a few moments, then he said, " I don't like that kind of joke, Crowley." Anhelonium makes you see visions in bright colours: its effects are surprising and exciting, but I found it made me feel sick afterwards so I took it only two or three times. Dreiser was eloquent under its influence and it didn't seem to make him feel sick. He lay on his back on a bed, side by side with a little English actor who was not taking kindly to the drug, and he described to us in detail, in that ponderous style which always weighed down his powerful genius, the coloured visions of landscape and of figures passing before him. He recited the deranged, fantastic invocations and adjurations—he Dreiserized them a good deal—that rang at intervals in his ears. It was like hearing one of his novels read aloud; but certainly with a difference. The little actor all the while continued to give punctuating groans and to be sick into the basin that he held clutched before him on his side of the bed, over which was the inscription "Jesus Wept". It was a hired room.

Afterwards Dreiser said to me, naïvely: "But isn't your friend—isn't that guy Crowley a bit of a crook?"

He met him again, though, and let him cook a curry luncheon at his "apartment". He enjoyed the curry, but Crowley once again provoked from him that look of wrath so familiar to anyone who knew Dreiser at all well. At a loss for the word for the young of swans, a word that he needed for a comparison in one of his long and rather involved disquisitions, he appealed to Crowley: "What *is* it? What would you call a young swan?"

"Why not call him Alfred?" said Crowley, tenderly. That, to Dreiser the serious Teuton, was an exasperating example of English frivolity. No doubt it strengthened his wish for our defeat in the first war. Crowley could not resist sticking his banderillas into the hide of this powerful bull.

This kind of irresponsible, light frivolity (English "nonsense"), under cover of a serious tone and manner, often appeared in Crowley's remarks. When a lady asked him what woman's college would be the best for her young daughter, he replied, with earnest gravity, "Radclyffe Hall." Such was the effect of Crowley's manner that, even though *The Well of Loneliness* had only recently been banned, the lady gratefully wrote down the name, not for a moment suspecting a joke. Frivolous with a difference was Crowley's reply when he was asked some forty years ago how one could sleep in Russia without being pestered by bed-bugs: " Shift the frontier." That was very much his own joke, in his own special grand manner, with his own gesture's special sweep. It was almost a religious joke because of its half-in-earnest indication of faith in the impossible. It was a large, fantastic, extravagant joke, all of a piece with his behaviour to money. Large and fantastic, too, was his declaration that he had a Five-Thousand-Year-Plan for civilizing America. " Sanguine, I know, but I'm always an optimist." He could be and often was extremely and characteristically funny in print as well as in conversation. In his play *Household Gods* " A boy? Then what am I ? " is, taken in its context, one of the most humorous exclamations in literature.

The extravagance, the excess that was so often in his humour was a deep, essential characteristic. His cult, his mania, one might say, was for excess in all directions: excess in writing, in drugging, in smoking the strongest cigars and pipe-tobaccos, and in drinking—though I never saw him drunk and never met anyone who had. His constitution was so amazingly tough that I believe he could have drunk with impunity a dozen or so of the cocktails made from his own recipe: " One part old brandy, one part old Kirsch, one third part absinthe, 6m Tabasco, spirit of ether to taste. Shake through ice." A letter to me of December, 1912, accepting my invitation to him to come and see me at Chiswick is in the same familiar vein of excess: "Fortunately I have kept together all my old Himalayan outfit, and shall be able to buy all I need in the course of the day, and start early tomorrow, if I can get mules." He much enjoyed the extravagances and exaggerations of W. S. Gilbert who was one of his favourite authors.

He had also a taste for practical jokes, and these too struck the note of excess. Some of them were very funny, as they happened, like the one that a brother-in-law of Crowley told me about. It was in Crowley's younger days when he was a wealthy man. He was living at Boleskine in the Highlands and was known as Lord Boleskine. At a much later date when living in Paris he called himself merely " Sir Aleister Crowley." I still have a visiting-card of his from that period, with a coronet on it too.

A Swiss visitor to Boleskine had been boasting to Crowley that he had shot all sorts of animals in all sorts of places. He was very keen, he said, on collecting heads to decorate his house at Geneva. He then asked, " What exactly is a haggis ? " " Ah ! " replied Crowley, " I am one of the very few people who would dare to answer such a question." (His voice and intonation were often remarkably like Winston Churchill's.) A haggis, he proceeded to explain, was in Scotland a " rogue " ram: just as in other parts of the world you have " rogue " elephants who are thrown out from the herd and live apart and are identified with the tribal fetish or tabu. Such animals are sacred. In Scotland, said Crowley, the haggis is sacred and most rare. When found, it must not be touched by any hand save that of the chief of the clan. The visitor was deeply interested and impressed.

As soon as he could, Crowley arranged for the purchase in Inverness of an old, decrepit ram which he had conveyed to Boleskine, and he tethered the animal among the rocks above his house. He then invited the sportsman to luncheon. The meal had hardly begun when one of the gillies, who had been carefully coached, rushed into the dining-room in great excitement and, falling on one knee, cried out, " My lord! My lord! There's a haggis on the hill! " Crowley at once took control. He and his ingenuous guest climbed the difficult rock face. Crowley gave a solemn warning not to venture too close, but the sportsman, now beyond all control, took aim from a distance and shot the " haggis " dead. Crowley gripped his arm. " As you value your life don't move from where you are! Only I may approach the sacred animal." He then ascended and with the help of the gillie carried down the poor dead old ram. " I risk the forfeit of my right to be paramount chief in Scotland," he explained, " for having dared for friendship's sake to commit such an outrage." The head of that ram perhaps still hangs with other trophies in the house at Geneva, over a gold-lettered inscription: " Haggis. Shot at Boleskine," and then the date. The only thing that went wrong was that the gillie made his dramatic entrance too early and Crowley had to go hungry until after the event. But is it possible that something else went wrong? That the Swiss gentleman knew what a haggis was all the time? That the joke was on Crowley?

Another well vouched for story of Crowley's practical joking takes less time to tell. He once followed close behind a stranger in the streets of New York, keeping step with him, and then he suddenly fell. Unconsciously enforced, the man just ahead fell too. He was supported and comforted by Crowley, and together they searched for the orange peel that wasn't there. On this occasion, and no doubt on others, Crowley combined the functions of magician and practical joker.

Some years more will have to pass before this man can be seen as a whole in true perspective. Such a view is always especially hard to take of anyone of whom adoration and vilification have both been carried to extremes. The difficulty is increased in Crowley's case because of the variety and the contradictoriness of the elements in his composition. I do not profess to be able to solve the enigma of his character and his actions. I am glad that he was himself and that

I knew him. My chief feeling about him is one of personal gratitude, for I have known very few who, as persons, have impressed me more or rewarded me more than he did. It is true that those who are notable for personality are not always notable for achievement; but this truth seems to me to be better illustrated by Frank Harris than by Aleister Crowley.

JOHN COWPER POWYS

I DOUBT if it has ever happened before that each one of three brothers has achieved distinction as a writer. Of the three Brontë sisters Charlotte and Emily achieved it, though this cannot be said so certainly of Anne. Today there is the remarkable family phenomenon of the two Sitwell brothers and their sister Edith. But I do not know of the existence, either now or in former times, of three brothers so distinguished in literature as are John Cowper Powys, Theodore Francis Powys, and Llewelyn Powys.

There was another brother—A. R. Powys, who died in 1936 and was for many years Secretary of the Society for the Protection of Ancient Buildings: he wrote some excellent books on architecture in a direct, truthful, and forcible style. Yet another, Littleton Powys, has published an autobiography of much interest, full of valuable commentary upon the other members of his family, a book affirming the values of life as he has experienced them, and of the values of Nature as seen through the loving eyes of a born countryman. Of the Powys sisters two have produced work of impressive individual quality: Gertrude Powys as a painter, exhibited in Paris and by The London Group;

Philippa Powys as a poet (" the only poet of our family," her brother Theodore has called her) and as the author of a remarkable, wild, poetic romance which was published by Constable under the title of *The Blackthorn Winter*. Another sister, Marian, is the leading expert on lace in America, and has written on that subject.

There is often some confusion between the three best known Powyses, so it may be as well to try to differentiate them. There are hardly any signs of relationship in the writings of these brothers: John, the eldest, does not write in the least like Theodore—indeed, no two writers could be less alike: neither did Llewelyn, the youngest, write in a way that suggests either Theodore or John. The work of each brother is strongly impressed by poetic feeling and by love of Nature; but it is not at all the same poetry; while love of Nature, too, is strained through the identity of each. For Theodore, for Llewelyn, for John, the meaning of poetry, the meaning of Nature, is something almost wholly different; it is determined by the writer's separate sense and separate spirit. From almost any single paragraph, taken at random from the work of any of the three, the identity of the author would at once be clearly seen. One of the surest signs of any author's value is his unmistakable stamping of himself upon what he writes. He may at the same time show derivation from others, it may be and it generally is possible to trace in him some quite well defined literary ancestry, but his own features will appear in unmistakable outline none the less, his own voice will always be heard. John Cowper Powys, essayist, poet, autobiographer, and novelist—but most notably autobiographer and novelist— shows inheritance from the Jacobean dramatists, from De Quincey, from Emily Brontë, from the fiercely romantic and fantastically imaginative writers of prose fiction at whom Jane Austen raised her satirical eyebrow in *Northanger Abbey:* Theodore Powys, novelist, short-story writer, and fabulist, often suggests John Bunyan in his style and religious feeling, and John Donne in his union of fantasy with realism: Llewelyn, essayist, biographer, author of books of travel, auto-biographical books, and one novel, shows in his style the influence of Charles Lamb, Walter Pater, and especially Robert Burton; and, in his thought, of the writers of the great humanist tradition, the writers who were lovers of life, such as Montaigne whom he called his master, and Rabelais. He was also influenced by Maupassant.

It is John himself, much more than anything that he has written, that, ever since I first met him more than fifty years ago, has enthralled me. I was then nineteen and he nearly twenty-nine. I had never met anyone at all like him: I could, indeed, hardly believe he was real. " If I were you," one of John's early admirers told him,

" I should think I was a god." A god whose persuading intonations were clear and loud, a young god, then, hard-fleshed, keen-boned, lean-bellied, in his human manifestation, not beautiful, with his loose aberrant mouth, his mousterian or simian forehead, " villainous low " or " like a girl's "—he has called it both the one and the other—his beaked nose and the heightened seemingly artificial colour of his " Red Indian " cheeks. Yet he did give an effect of beauty, notably when he was lecturing, but not only then; and it was beauty of a transfixing power for those who saw and heard him. He was, and is, full of life, full of beliefs, full of the power to communicate his abundance. When we first met I realized this as his greatest value. " I am come that ye may have life, and that ye may have it more abundantly." Those words often came to me when I was with John Cowper in the early days.

He had then published nothing but lecture syllabuses and two thin volumes of disregarded verse, written nothing else but the beginning of a novel and a book on Keats, neither of which has ever been published. It was only as a lecturer that he was known, and only to University Extension audiences. His eloquence was as exciting and persuasive in private as it was in public; and he was the most powerful public speaker that I have ever heard. Eloquence, imagination, force of life, and a complete freedom from the usual cautions and conventions and deferences and meannesses were what most strongly impressed me in John Cowper when I met him first. Also, very importantly, he had then, as always, to an extraordinary degree, the gift of drawing out the mental and emotional resources of anyone he met, even though these were resources that they could not draw out for themselves. If there was any validity in anyone, he was the magnet for it. " He makes you feel you're important," a rather humble and diffident friend of mine once said of him, and that was true, for he drew out whatever there might be of any sort of importance, or of any possibility of importance.

By his talk and his companionship and sympathy he stimulated, he intensified; he gave exaltation and incitement without effort, by natural force. When I said that Frank Harris was the best talker I had ever met, John Cowper did not come to my mind, because these two men, in their talk as in everything else, were so utterly different, their eloquence and their " spirit of life " different altogether, and their humour. John has his own humour, much of it, but no wit. No Powys, except sometimes Theodore, is witty. It would be impossible for anyone who knows John well to describe him as " a good talker ". There would be something irrelevant, inadequate, inept, in such a description. What he says has the effect of an incantation, of the weaving of a spell.

His friends and brothers—especially Llewelyn

—often resented the generosity with which he lent himself to the invasions of acquaintances or strangers, the magnanimity with which he would unreservedly accept even the most tedious and inconvenient people. We didn't want to share him with them: we jealously wanted to keep him almost entirely to ourselves. In the early summer of 1912 I was in Venice with my first wife and John and Llewelyn. Ralph Shirley, cousin to the Powyses, had given us an introduction to Frederick Rolfe who called himself Baron Corvo and became, after his death, the subject of A. J. A. Symons's book, *The Quest for Corvo*. He was then enjoying a rare few weeks of prosperity. He was living well: he had his private gondola, beautifully manned. Because of Shirley's relationship to John and Llewelyn, he called us " the nephews ": and no uncle could have entertained us more liberally. Nor more assiduously: Rolfe was too assiduous. Even if he had been much less so Llewelyn and I would have found him an unwelcome intruder upon our hours with John. A little Corvo would have been all very well, indeed it would have been quite agreeable, but there was too much: even John wanted to evade him after a while. I remember him saying, apprehensively, " He'll be wanting to introduce us to some of those sham Italian countesses he talks of," and although Llewelyn replied, " Why not? I'd rather like to meet a few sham Italian countesses," he almost at once began again entreating John to put a stop to Corvo, at whatever cost. Left to himself, John could never have done it. He was too kind. Indeed his sensitiveness to other people's feelings could be almost morbid. It was only because we egged him on so pertinaciously that he managed to screw himself to the sticking-point and relieve us for good of Corvo's pressure. It was a great effort to him, and he did it very badly, comically badly. The end came at the bottom of the Campanile. Corvo asked when our next meeting was to be. " Tomorrow? "—" We're engaged, I'm afraid, for tomorrow." John, the eldest, was our spokesman. " The day after? "—" I'm afraid we're engaged then too."—" Well, perhaps Thursday? " At that point John lost his nerve. " We're *engaged!* " he shouted. " All the time! Up to the hilt! Engaged! *Up to the hilt!* " Corvo turned on his heel with one of the swiftest movements I have ever seen and shot away from us across the Piazza. John's brutality, as Rosebery said of Cromwell's at Drogheda, may be extenuated though it cannot be justified. " There was great provocation." Corvo was a learned and a clever man, often interesting and individual; but his vanity was excessive, he was without humour, and he could be as pretentiously affected as much of his writing is. We could not let him go on getting in the way between us and John.

Mrs. Humphry Ward was once sent packing by John with an equal finality, but she was not there, she was dead, she was dismissed only from a lecture. Llewelyn, lecturing in America, was compelled to take her as a subject. In dismay and despair he turned over the pages of one of her novels, ejaculating, " But it's awful! It's terrible! What a woman! " John came to the rescue. Addressing Llewelyn and me and a stenographer, he gave as eloquent, as brilliant and as entertaining a lecture on Mrs. Ward as though he had been addressing an audience of a thousand. When the typed copy of the lecture came in, it wasn't long enough. So John took up the tale of Mrs. Ward again. After a while he grew restive. He was not at all in the mood for Mrs. Ward that morning. He came to the peroration.

" But, ladies and gentlemen," he announced, " it is, after all, not so much as a social thinker, as a novelist, as a mistress of English prose, that Mrs. Ward will be remembered. It is rather for qualities of a more personal, a much more personal, a much more intimate kind." He proceeded to an impassioned eulogy of those qualities, which it may be inadvisable to transcribe. " In a word," he concluded, " in a word, ladies and gentlemen, in one word, she is, she is a—in brief, she is a ——".

" Do you think there's enough now without that? " Llewelyn anxiously enquired.

It may well be because I have known John

Cowper so well for the last half century and not only because I don't like long books that I have always found difficulty in reading his novels, or at any rate in reading them all through. I miss his looks and voice, miss all the tokens of the intimacy of his relationship to myself and to others of the company, I miss those accidental breaks and diversions that relieve and refresh the meetings of friends. So John's writing too often becomes, for me, a mere substitute for his presence, a second or third best, and I find faults in it of which I am never aware in himself as companion. Most friends of most writers have no doubt had this experience in more or less degree. I have never had it in anything like the same degree or kind when reading the writings of others of my friends. But that is not to say that John Cowper does not " put his genius into his work ": he does, he is there himself, often fully; it is only that I cannot fully receive him through his written words, even though I know that they express him, that they have his own controlling and various imaginative power.

He is first of all an imaginative writer, an inhabitant of regions created by his own imagination, his own fantasy. He is a teller of wild, extravagant, even frenzied and often preposterous tales. He writes for his own satisfaction: to give expression to his illusions about life. He writes without care for form or style, without, indeed, taking any pains whatsoever in the usual literary sense. " I am not an artist," he has repeatedly affirmed. Both Llewelyn and Theodore, contrastingly, are careful craftsmen, rewriting often many times over; it may even be said that Llewelyn's earlier work suffered from excess of care: that, before he attained the freedom, ease, and naturalness of his later style, with its delicate, vibrant power, the effect produced was sometimes of a writing too conscious, too studied, too " literary ", and even, now and again, not free from " preciousness ". There has assuredly never been any " preciousness " in the writing of John Cowper. He writes what is really impromptu speech. This is his natural medium. He spoke always without notes of any kind: if he had taken any with him on to the platform, I am sure he would have forgotten all about them. He invented his lectures as he went on with them, just as he invented his novels, without premeditation. This was the fascination of his public speaking—that you knew that he didn't know what was coming next, and at the same time you knew that whatever was to come was sure to be provocative and exciting, not in the least suggestive of the mind or the nature of anyone else. He could hold an audience for an hour and a half. " *Super eos stillabat eloquium.*" John's eloquence did not always drop with the effect of dew; it was more often like lava. His fault as a speaker was the same fault that might be found with him as a writer. He went on too long. Even his eloquence and passion could not continue to bind an audience when he went on speaking, as he sometimes did, for more than an hour and a half. So, to me, it is with his thousand-page novels. How often I have wished that someone would make an abridgement of those novels for readers like myself. Skilfully and sympathetically done, it might strengthen their value. The excessive length of them as they stand is, however, a defect of that very quality of their author's which is his prime impulse. He writes to satisfy his own need, and to *go on doing it*. This *full* satisfaction is what he puts first, not the reader's power of endurance.

But these personally biased observations of mine must not deter any stranger to John Cowper's writings from seeking to become familiar with them. I should be sorry to be the cause of such a deprivation. Only a critic bound by academic limitations will feel that this fault or defect, or indeed any one of John's faults or defects, outweighs the vividness and power of his imagination and of the expression that he gives to it. The impromptu speech that floods his pages may lack artistic restraint, it may be wilful and self-indulgent and excessive; but, again and again, in company with all this exuberance and anarchy, there is the creative ardour and force of genius. Reflecting that John Cowper writes, as it were, by word of mouth, one might trace his literary ancestry back to the wandering story-tellers of the earliest days of our literature. But his are not the simple heroic sagas of ancient times. He is from one point of view an extremely modern writer, whose novels are records of strange, twisted, complex, some would say " evil " digressions from what most people think of as normal and natural human relationships. These novels—*Jobber Skald*, *Maiden Castle*, *Porius*, *The Inmates*—are full of fantastic heavens and fantastic hells of states of being, and there is more of hell than there is of heaven. In reading them I have often suffered exasperation, impatience, resentment; but, even though against my wish, judgment, nature, prejudice or what you will, I have found myself carried on by a tide that I cannot resist: I have become, in an unexpected moment, as it were initiated. I have read on; with a sense of unearthly revelation of the kind that comes from visions induced by opium or by hashish. There is, in our time, no writer who produces the same sort of phantasmagoric effect as John Cowper Powys. His faults are flagrant: formlessness, repetitions, intolerable *longueurs*, false rhetoric, " waste lands " that may encroach largely, chapter after chapter; gross and ridiculous absurdities, very provocative to the parodist: but with all this there is sure genius: a genius comparable in force with that of Webster or of Ford. In all his novels there is evidence of it. In *Morwyn*, a novel of which the main purpose is an attack upon vivisectionists who are shown as the sole inhabitants of yet another hell conceived by this egregious superfantast—even in this perhaps the most wayward and undisciplined of all his works, there are passages of the same authentic inspiration that gives its own singular life to *Wolf Solent* and to *A Glastonbury Romance*, or to the more recent vast historical novel which he wrote about his ancestor Owen Glendower. In some important respects, indeed, John does not a little remind us of Owen Glendower as portrayed in Shakespeare's *Henry the Fourth*.

It is difficult to illustrate him by quotation, either from his stories or from the essays in which he stimulates himself by contact with the writers of the past. In both, and in his books about things in general, the effects are cumulative. There are few sudden revealing shafts of light: there is none of that brevity which is the soul of epigram and aphorism no less than of wit. But when you have read the whole of his essay* on, say, Dante, that poet's genius and its vices have been set for you under a new kind of illumination, however fitful and partial it may sometimes be. Any work of John Cowper's is memorable *as a whole*. Its effect is rather like that of impressionistic oil painting.

I wrote to him asking if he could suggest any passages for quotation, and he replied no: a good reason for this negative reply being that he can never bring himself to read anything that he has written. " I never can bear opening

* In *The Pleasures of Literature*. Thomas Hardy thought the essay on Shelley John's best and liked the one on Dante "much the least ".

any book of mine," are his actual words. I think
he must be the only writer of any age or country
who has never read a line of his own except
when writing it; though possibly this is true also
of Dostoevsky. I can think of no other of whom
it could be reasonably guessed. There are many
significances in the fact that John admires and
delights in Dostoevsky more than in any other
modern author. Significant, too, is the reason
that he has given me for his incapacity to read
his own works. " It is partly, I think, because
being an actor and self-conscious through and
through and being really scared of thinking of
myself or facing myself, I always run away—in
fact, my whole life is a running away from
myself. I live by sensations, but the ' I ' enjoying
those sensations is a funny almost impersonal
sort of camera-bird spreading its wings in a
second if attention is turned from the sensations
upon it! In this you see how little of an artist
I am and how different from Llewelyn and
Theodore whose style is the natural and inevitable
expression of their personalities. I have no style
—save purple patches à la De Quincey. I *hate*
the idea of my ' personality ', whereas Llewelyn
said to me once before he got his fame, ' I have
nothing but my personality '. What I like far
best myself in my writings are my longest novels
and romances because I tell myself stories then
and just ramble on, losing myself and my
' personality ' in those I'm writing about—just
exactly the same delicious escape from reality as

when I read exciting stories of the sort I especially like."

His writing, then, so important a part of his life, is the same " running away ". He writes to escape from objective reality, to escape from himself. He summons all the resources of his powerful romantic imagination to enable him to do this as completely as he can. But he can never wholly escape from himself through his imagination or his fantasy or through his writings about other writers or about the general concerns of life, because he is always there in everything that he views or imagines. He is an intensely subjective writer: everything that he writes of is strained through himself. All the characters of his novels are, you might say, John Cowper-ized. This does not mean that they are not endowed with life. They are living, though they are by no means always real. In the peculiar fantasy of their creation there is life, as there is—of course with much difference—in the characters of Dickens, who is another writer for whom John Cowper has an enthusiastic devotion.

In the letter from which I have been quoting he speaks of his " invented " characters—a word that detached, objective writers would never use in this connection.

" I think myself that my most lasting work is in my invented characters in my long books and in the excitement of the adventures that they have, and after that in certain little descriptions (*not* the purple patches De Quincey ones!) of inanimates like posts and stumps and stones rather in Bewick style, and perhaps also, not so much poetized as very carefully noted, certain unusual effects of mists. . . . But here over this blooming Nature business I am so ridiculously ignorant that I make the most incredible mistakes about—well, say about the moon and where the hell it is! and about which way it rises or sets or pokes out its ' silvery ' horns!

" But what I would like you to stress is the fact that I have only one very very strong principle, conviction, or moral opinion, namely that vivisection should be abolished. On that one single point I am austere, fanatical, puritanical, and as fierce as an early Christian. Another point you might stress is that I don't like the idea of God and that I am instinctively hostile to love and to Narcissist craving for love, *personal* love. That is why I like to try to be a Polytheist and a Pluralist à la William James and Walt Whitman."

John, then, believes in many gods, he breaks God up into little bits, he believes in lots of little gods, nice simple little unpretending " common or garden " gods, some of them. Whereas Llewelyn believed in no gods at all; and to Theodore God is an idea that dominates his writings. All three of them are heretics, as might be expected, since both their father and their grandfather were clergymen. One friend

of John's described him as an "actor-priest",
but he has none of that priestly or pontifical
æsthetic-moral unction, as he calls it, which
distinguishes a certain contemporary cult.

Of all his books it may be that future readers
will regard his *Autobiography* as the most important. I hope they will, because it is my
favourite. If he writes in order to escape from
himself, why, you may ask, did he write an
autobiography? Perhaps because the best of all
escapes from oneself is to write about oneself; just
as the best escape from inhibitions and "com-
plexes" is to bring them to the light. Facing
the realities of himself John Cowper exorcized
them by writing his autobiography, that extraordinary and, for him, extraordinarily short
volume of only six hundred and fifty-two pages.
"Everybody I meet seems to want to assert their
ego," he writes in it. "'I! I! I!' they all cry.
No one seems to get the depraved pleasure I get
from turning my 'I' into thin air and helping
my friends' 'I' to swell and swell until it's a
regular balloon." Such pleasure is, of course,
intensely egoistic, and, as will have already
appeared, highly characteristic of John
Cowper.

For those desiring a saturation with the
quintessence of John, the *Autobiography* is the very
thing. "I am perfectly aware," he writes
towards the end of it, "how indignant—on my

behalf—my closest friends will be over this
autobiography of mine.   But fortunately if ' truth
is to be served ' I have an invaluable organ of
research in myself which is more powerful than
any scientific microscope.   I refer to *my sacred
and holy malice*, my wicked and creative-destructive
joy in bringing down the dignified ' John ' in
me and exalting the living pierrot of my soul.
And what, when you really come down to it, is
the use of these clever sophisticated ' Memoirs '
of tedious dignitaries, who never once let you
see the shivering, jerking, scratching, crying,
groaning, God-alone-sees-me nerve of their
central ' Libido ' ? . . .

   " Now where my own spiritual sincerity comes
in, is that part of my soul follows close behind
my ' childishness ', close behind all my manias,
all my superstitions, all my peculiarities, like an
exultant demon-falcon, shrieking and fluttering,
and deriving a voluptuous pleasure from catching
myself acting like a sentimentalist or an idiot.
I even think sometimes, when I consider how
my deepest impulses are neither exactly sadistic
nor masochistic or mystical or theatrical or quite
sane or quite mad, that there ought to be coined
a completely new formula for what I am; *and
perhaps this is true of every living soul*.   In fact I
would modestly offer to students of abnormality
the word ' Cowperist ' to describe what I am. . . .
But this I do at least know of myself: I combine
an extremely quick and mercurial intelligence
with a lean, primordial, bony, gaunt neanderthal

simplicity. My nimble wit is in fact the Ariel-
like slave of my Caliban primitiveness, and its
deadly and thaumaturgic champion against the
world."

This is, I think, as brief, as compact a piece
of self-exposition as John Cowper has given us.

He is by his nature predestined to auto-
biographical writing. He certainly does, in his
own way, " assert his ego " in his *Autobiography*,
with the result that it is one of the most remarkable and exciting books of its kind ever written.
" One can rarely tell the truth about others and
never about oneself," and how far John Powys
is truthful about himself who can tell? At least
it can be said that to tell the whole truth, without
reserve, was his aim—an aim that was in no way
obstructed by his avowed method of treating
himself as if he were one of his own fictional
characters, with a touch of caricature. He shows
himself none the less as truly and as fully as he
can, he tells everything, however damaging it
may be, however much it may stir resentment,
hostility, derision and contempt. Rousseau was
not more candid. Neither vanity nor false
humility has been allowed to falsify John
Cowper's self-portrayal, any more than shame
or reticence has been allowed to falsify it by
omission. He has no more written himself down
than he has written himself up; even though he
does say that he has risked making himself out

more of a rascal and more of a fool than his friends have supposed him to be.

If a writer tries to write the whole truth about himself he cannot observe what is known as " decent reticence ", and so he is at once accused of " exhibitionism ". Why should he seek to rebut such a charge? His chief purpose has been to exhibit himself. In any autobiography the author *is* the " exhibit ", he is, if not the only " exhibit ", at any rate the most important one, the one that justifies the book.

In John Cowper Powys's *Autobiography* he is not of course the only character. No one can write of himself without writing also of those who have been near to him. John writes of Theodore and Llewelyn, of the other brothers in his large and peculiarly cohesive family, of his father, and of his friends. He holds a mirror up to them, the John Cowper mirror in which you see him as well.

Love of endowing Nature with a queer sort of human consciousness, his own sort, is another of John's many idiosyncrasies. His " animism " is animism with a difference, a " Cowperist " difference. Sometimes he shows this sentience in Nature as sinister and malignant. In a letter that he wrote me many years ago from Virginia, certainly with no thought of publication, he describes " a marsh by a sea-estuary among reeds and black decaying tree-trunks and indescribable mud—and on the other side of the water black cypresses. . . . The place heaved and palpitated with the life of putrescence like a horrible great heart. . . . It was the cradle of all the physical nightmares that prey on morbid nerves. It heaved with horrible death-in-life . . . with forbidden life. It was like black blood breeding *snakes*. . . . A dead tree as tall as a mast had a heron's nest against the sunset, and great shrieking cries of some sort of fish-hawks died over the water."

This strikes the horrific black-magical or black-romantic note of later eighteenth-century invention, and of Edgar Allan Poe—another of John's favourite writers. There is also in it a suggestion of some moods of Byron, as well as the moods which often controlled Emily Brontë.

Aged now nearly eighty, in his retreat among the Welsh mountains, John Cowper continues to write. He has called writing his greatest pleasure and has said that it will be his greatest pleasure until he dies.

THEODORE FRANCIS POWYS

THE world of Theodore Francis Powys is not John Cowper's world in any detail, in any intimation. He is no less strongly individual in his writing than either John or Llewelyn; but again I would say that there is no literary kinship between him and Llewelyn, or between him and John. In a recent work on English Literature notice of the three brothers was compressed into a single sentence, which commented on the love of Nature that they share. It is true that they are all three countrymen born and bred; each is profoundly aware of Nature; each has, you might say, a religion of Nature: but their awareness and their religion can be only contrasted. To Theodore the most important discovery in life is, and always has been, God. From early youth he has been a searcher after God, a meditator upon Him, upon the God that he calls " the Life that is within you ".

I have always counted Theodore Powys and Aleister Crowley as my two most religious friends; differing of course often most widely in religious sense and belief, though not so widely in their conception of God. Theodore's view of Nature in relation to God does not, however, at all suggest Crowley. The chief service of Nature, to him, is that it brings him thoughts upon God, that it brings God nearer. The first book of his that was ever printed is *An Interpretation of Genesis* and is a dialogue between Zetetes, the Searcher, and the Lawgiver of Israel; it looks like a Church-pew book: his second book was *The Soliloquy of a Hermit*, later entitled *Soliloquies of a Hermit*. Both these books are religious. " Man," he writes in the *Soliloquy*, " is a collection of atoms through which pass the moods of God—a terrible clay picture, tragic, frail, drunken, but always deep rooted in the earth, always with claws holding on to his life while the moods pass over him and change his face and his life every moment. The people of the earth are clay pieces that the moods of God kindle into life."

And again: " I know how men move under the shadow of the moods of God, and I know how I move. Some try to hide in the Garden, and some try to hide in the beast's belly. I have tried to hide amongst grassy hills; but the moods of God have hunted me out. . . . As I could not hide from God, I tried to hide from myself, and watch the moods as they pass by. To believe in God and not to believe in yourself is the first duty of a priest." " All human laws are made to trap and snare God's movements; men are always trying to get at ease with themselves and away from His terrible ways."

Nature, to Theodore, means God. " It is the spring, and the apple-blossom is beautiful because He is there in it. To love Him is the only good thing in this world. It does not matter if He is true; He is beyond all Truth. All things have breath in Him: I feel Him in the earth. When I hammer at the rocks and break away fossils that have been there for thousands of years, I am only going a little way into His love. When I look up in the night and see the light that has left a star hundreds of years ago, I can only see a little way into His love. His love is a terrible love— terrible and deep, hard for a man to bear; I have lived in it, I know it." " I see the awful Majesty of the Creator come into our own Grange mead, and lie down amidst a joyous crowd of buttercups and red clover."

It is impossible to write about God without restatements; but these restatements are not those of any other writer. In this book, as in all his books, the style is extremely simple, with the power of simplicity. " This is what I care to remember. I can feel now the warmth of a perfect day in June; I can see the bugloss on the cliff, growing in little patches of blue below the white chalk. And I remember a night in winter when I saw a white lamb lying quite dead under a clear moon. I see now the rough old black dog, blind of one eye, that used to be asleep on the green in the dog-days that are past; and its master, a wild old man with a great stride and long beard who was always hammering up pig-styes."

But Theodore will be remembered as a novelist and as a short-story writer rather than for his direct expressions of his searchings or his faith. These searchings, this faith, have generated his novels, his stories, his fables; in which he has expressed not only his sense of God, but, more variously and more notably than in his first two books, he has communicated his special vision of life, a vision both tragic and humorous, of men and women, of human desires, of the ways of human lives, of good and of evil. He is a born mystic, but he is a materialist-mystic, and he is full of the most amazing fantasies. The world of his novels and stories is not, in the literal sense, the real world; it is a world set, as it were, at some removes from reality, but always with a true correspondence to reality, a symbolic or allegorical correspondence. There is often a strange suggestion of medievalism, of Gothic art, about his work; his characters are sometimes like gargoyles, sometimes like sculptured saints, but they have the same significant, interpretive relation to actual men and women that medieval images have; they bear the same illumination. No writer could be less contemporaneous; his sense of mystery, his awe, his sense of good and evil, of beauty and of horror, were utterly foreign to almost all varieties of literary taste in the earlier years of the present century. That was why he could never, during those years, get his books published. It needed the first world war, with its change of orientations, its destruction of old views and values and its revelation of new ones, to clear the way for any general appreciation of the writings of T. F. Powys. The same catastrophe was needed for the revival of appreciation of the mysticism, the fantasy, and the realism of a writer who is T. F. Powys's kinsman both in the literal and the figurative sense, John Donne.

My first contacts—I cannot call them meetings —with Theodore I hardly remember. I was eight and he was fourteen when he came to my father's school at Aldeburgh. I don't even remember his punching my head, as he says he once did; it could not have been at all a severe punch. He was sent to my father's school because his mother and mine were friends in girlhood. That friendship is the origin of my intimacy with the Powys family. It was not until the year before I met John Cowper, when I was eighteen and Theodore twenty-four, that I stayed with him at his farm at Sweffling in Suffolk. That was the beginning of my interest in him and his writing, the beginning too of my interest in wine, for he gave me good Burgundy. He was already writing in the vein which was so many years later to make his reputation, though not with the technique: already he was suffering his profound obsession with the ideas of God and Death. In those Sweffling days he wrote a dialogue between himself and God. " Can you see everything? "—" I can."—" Can you see Sally? " Details were given of Sally's girlish occupations from moment to moment, and then: " I do not think you would like to see what she is doing now," said God. Of Bunyan no doubt T. F. Powys is a spiritual descendant, but that he is also a descendant of Swift is proved not only by that early dialogue, which he long ago destroyed.

During the next twenty years I read in manuscript—literally " manuscript ", for it was all written in his own careful hand, as legible as print—almost everything that he wrote. My admiration grew: I was more and more convinced that he was a really remarkable writer, a unique solitary. I tried, as others did, to interest publishers and writers in his work, but with no success. Those manuscripts always came back to him. In 1908 I shared with John Cowper the small expenses of the private printing of the *Interpretation of Genesis*: in 1916, when Theodore was forty, Arnold Shaw, the American lecture-manager of John Cowper and myself, published *The Soliloquy of a Hermit* in New York. In 1918 this *Soliloquy* was published in London by Andrew Melrose who announced his intention of publishing *Mr. Tasker's Gods*, but thought better of it.

It was not until 1923, when Theodore was forty-seven and his manuscripts had been accumulating for more than two decades that, thanks to Stephen Tomlin and David Garnett, Chatto & Windus published *The Left Leg*. Then, very soon, Douglas Goldring got Theodore an American publisher. In the same year Chatto & Windus brought out *Black Bryony*, and other novels and stories of Theodore's during the following years, in rapid succession. No wonder the succession was rapid: these books had all been written years before; it was only a matter of taking them out of the drawer. Continued discouragement over so many years never stopped Theodore from writing: he went on just the same. I believe he would have written exactly what he has, no more and no less, even though not a line of his had ever got into print. Now, unlike his brother John, he writes nothing, has written nothing for the last fifteen years or so, although there have been Selections and reprints. " I am out of business," he says, and he has moods when he talks of " those silly books ", meaning not only his own, but all books. Very rarely he writes a letter. In the Dorset village where he now lives with his wife and daughter, he, aged seventy-seven, chops wood, brings in coal, rakes ashes, and keeps the fires in; he reads a little, takes a two or three mile walk along the same road every day, sees his friends now and again, and goes to church in the evenings except on Sundays. His house is next to the churchyard, and he speaks of a little girl who is buried there and who died in 1810 as though she were his living next-door neighbour. As the churchyard ground is raised, Theodore's head is about on a level with hers and only a few yards away when he is lying in bed. Like the old Jews, Theodore believes in God without believing in survival after death. But he does believe in a sort of survival *in* death, and that is why he can say " He's in this grave," and really mean it. He thinks the dead have some sort of consciousness, and a rather pleasant sort, under the ground. Perhaps rather like the consciousness of plants. He thinks that cremation is " cheating your friends "; he might have added that it is cheating yourself.

Theodore Powys did not remain a farmer for more than a few years; but he did not lose money at farming. He did not succeed, either: he kept himself, and not much more. Soon he came to feel that farming, for him, was a waste of time: it did not interest him enough. The life of a " hermit " in the West Country would suit him better, and (he may also have reflected) give him more time to write. His father allowed sixty pounds a year to his unmarried sons, a hundred pounds a year to the married ones. Theodore decided to live on the bachelor allowance and did so until he gained the hundred a year by his marriage in 1905. It must be remembered that money was then worth three or four times as much as it is now.

In those days, and much later, too, Theodore's meditations upon God and death used always to fill him with profound melancholy; but now, as he himself has said, " I have lost my melancholy". He said that as though he were rather sorry to miss his lifelong companion. During his later years he showed some other changes. I would not say that he is more assured than he was before he was recognized as a writer, for he was always that outwardly, however subject to inward fears and misgivings he may have been. His recognition, with the contacts that it inevitably brought, his marriage and his having children, have naturally made him less of a hermit. He talks a good deal more than he used to; that may be partly because he is older. Since he talks as much like himself as he always has, this change is a good one.

Although Theodore's behaviour to life is rather different now, he has not really changed. When with him, I always have the strong illusion that we are both twenty, thirty, forty, or fifty years younger. He is to me just as he was at Sweffling, at Studland, at East Chaldon, or when he visited me at Aldeburgh or Cambridge. In his talk he is less intransigent, less violent than he sometimes was in the old days: one could say that he had " mellowed ". He always had urbanity, but he has even more of it now.

In the earlier years of this century he wore a

heavy moustache and looked astonishingly like
Nietzsche. Looking back, I see him as a heavily
built young man with grey melancholy eyes.
His manners were courteous to the point of what
seemed to me an ironic deference. Always he
was a countryman; I well recall the sharply
contrasting effect that his rural not rustic
appearance made when he dined in my rooms at
Cambridge. Among those lively young undergraduates, those bright birds of rejoicing plumage,
there was a brown and earthy soberness in
Theodore's aspect. His talk was in contrast, too:
slow, rather timid sometimes, but ripe and bear-
ing authority. No one could have been more
alien to our kind of cleverness with its conscious
precocity, our dapper " wit ", our studied French
colloquialisms, our " undergraduate chatter ",
which was the phrase that Theodore used later
in life when talking about one of his celebrated
contemporaries. His ironical humour fed silently
on us, I am sure.

At no time of his life has Theodore tried
to be witty or epigrammatic, and I have
rarely heard him use a bawdy word. He
was as much a foreigner to our slick young
bawdry as he was to the whole technique of our
conversation. He was not aloof, though. When
the slight ripples of one of our " daring " jests
were spent, with how decorous a gesture he
would cast in those same waters, but far deeper
than any of our plummets could sound, his own
grave word. There would be a moment's

silence, then those tortuous and often sinister coils of Theodore's humour would come obscurely to our view, and we would laugh. But I think we all of us felt we were laughing more on the wrong side of our mouths than on the right. Sometimes he made us feel even a little aghast, although we would never have admitted it.

No wonder he has never been a popular writer. But he himself was popular with us, in spite of those devastating moments, and I don't think there was one of us who did not feel admiration and even respect for him: which, considering what we were, is saying a good deal. No one, however remote from him, could have resented or disliked him, so courteous was his manner, so sensitive his tact. He had always the air of being greatly entertained in our company, and he would laugh most heartily at jokes in French of which I knew that he understood not a single word.

When he was with his closer friends, Theodore was less formal, less guarded, particularly if it was late at night and he had drunk well. He had a natural flair for good drink and he lovingly relished the hot punch which our older friend, the oldest and best friend of the Powys family, Bernard O'Neill, used to mix for us with such art, but he never drank immoderately. I remember one late night at Cambridge when a brilliant young Indian undergraduate had been of the company. We other undergraduates had a high opinion of this man's intellect: naturally,

96

because, being of his race, he was as mature as a man of thirty. We could not realize that what impressed us was his wide reading and his assimilative power, and that there was little that was original and nothing that was creative about his mind. After he and the other guests had left, I expressed admiration of him, O'Neill showed kindly interest, Theodore was silent. Rising to go to bed an hour or so later, " As for these Indians," he said, " I think they ought all to be shot ".

No reader of his novels will be surprised to learn that the contemplation of acts of violence gave him a strange satisfaction. More than a generation later he was reading a book about Oriental despots. He told me about one of them who was, he said, " friendly to killing ". It is difficult to imagine anyone else using that phrase. In Theodore's tones there could be implications of incredible inhumanity. In his mind there were always the same realistic fantasies of savagery and cruelty, of horror and evil, that are recorded in so many of his stories*, and in himself the same deep gentleness and benevolence, the same sensitiveness, and the same humour. " What do you think," I once asked him, " of the idea that if a girl doesn't love a man, love will grow with marriage? " " The only thing that will grow," said Theodore, " is horns." " Church, Navy, Army, Bar," I had once angrily declaimed. " Our only gentlemanly ' pro-

* *A Suet Pudding* in *Bottle's Path* is one of these.

97

fessions'! "—" Liars, murderers, and thieves," was Theodore's tranquil comment. He talked as he wrote, and to his daily vision the world has always been the world of his novels, set at its fixed remove from reality, peopled by gargoyles or saints.

When I think of Theodore Powys as the one great Gothic seer, the one great Gothic artist of our time, and as among the few earlier twentieth-century writers of great and lasting importance, I sometimes wonder if I am biased by knowing him so well. Yet, though my view is not widely shared, I am not alone in it. In spite of his not being a popular writer, some of his books, because of his prestige, have been published in popular editions, and he has been translated into French, German, Italian, and Russian. The appeal of his work is not only to a coterie. To a minority, yes; but, so I believe, to a minority that will exist through coming centuries.

There is a kind of creative genius that seems to be " pure ", unmixed with talent, or obliterating talent, putting it out of view. Even after knowing him for fifty years I can still be startled by the sense of this kind of genius when in Theodore's company. With him you have, suddenly, un-expectedly, the sense of being " in the Presence ". This is something that I have had fully with only three others—George Meredith, James Joyce, and Jacob Epstein; not because of anything that they were saying or doing, but because of what they were. With other men of power and distinction—such as Thomas Hardy, W. B. Yeats, Somerset Maugham, Aldous Huxley, Arnold Bennett—I have never had quite the same feeling. Was it, I have wondered, because the genius in these men was not " pure ", because it was not only " mixed with " but sometimes kept under by talent, so that, when you met them, it was the talent, the talent's distinction by which alone you were impressed? Or because their genius was remote from their outward selves? But of course the validities and invalidities of one's own receptive faculty have to be taken into account in such a matter. Taken into account, too, when one is much or little impressed by another kind of genius, a genius of personality in those who have little or none in their work.

" I like best," Theodore has said, " a story about ordinary people, and then, for something odd to come in." This is a mark of his own stories. They are about people who are in essentials ordinary, for all the strangeness of their presentation. Rebecca West once remarked that, to Theodore, Old Testament characters (including, she may have meant, God) were the villagers of East Chaldon, and there is truth in this. To Theodore the age-old, unvarying characteristics of human beings are what is important. Before my first visit to Montacute Vicarage, where most of the family then were with their father and mother, I could get nothing out of Theodore by way of preparation for that momentous occasion. "Well, Willie, of course, he's a boy," I remember him saying. "My brother John," he once said. "He has those three women, and he doesn't get very much from them."—"What three women?" I asked.—"His wife and those two servants." Theodore would seem to simplify all individuals into men, women, boys and girls: good or bad, "honest cods", or "scurvy" (those were the Rabelaisian expressions that he used then), but not much else. When Theodore talked about people, they seemed, as he spoke, to resolve themselves into their pure essentials and become eating, drinking, sleeping, copulating, dung-making animals. I have never heard him describe anyone as an individual in conversation.

What happens to those ordinary or typical characters in Theodore's stories is certainly often odd enough. Readers of *Mr. Weston's Good Wine* will remember how time stood still in the village inn. Fantastic and grotesque things happen; lovely things and things that are horrible: for the intensity of Theodore's perception of what is lovely and of what is good involves an equal intensity of perception of what is ugly and repellent, as in the horrible Mr. Tasker and in the scene in which his father is eaten by the pigs. Theodore's loving and tender, and one might almost say pious embrace of good necessitates his savage, ferocious, perhaps vindictive revelation of evil, the saturation of his consciousness with evil and with evil's horror. In his books there is poison, and there is balm.

The most important of his novels are, I think, *Mr. Weston's Good Wine* and *Unclay*. Both are allegories: Mr. Weston, the wine-merchant with his light wine of love and dark wine of death, is God: the chief character in *Unclay* is Death, the tailor. To know how Mr. Weston is God, and how John Death is Death, it is necessary to read the books. The appearances of both these figures are contrived with Theodore's own subtle craft and goblin-like or gnome-like humour. Of equal importance with *Mr. Weston* and *Unclay* are the *Fables*, republished in a Phœnix edition under the title of *No Painted Plumage*. Theodore may well be right in thinking this the best of all his books. The *Fables*, as one would expect, are about inanimate things and beasts, as well as about human beings. Each of them reveals common events and characters as Theodore most uncommonly sees them: each shows us some aspect of usual human experience through his special vision, and each abounds in his own responses, his own intimations. The fable is peculiarly well suited to Theodore's way of writing. Indeed there is something, often a good deal, of the nature of a fable in all his novels and stories. But, in his *Fables* proper, his fantasy and his wisdom, his sense of the magic and the mystery of human life and of the world's ordering have freer range.

I am more inclined to quote again from

Theodore than to go on writing about him. Although his effects are cumulative, this does not make quotation so unsatisfactory as it does in the case of his brother John. Quotation can give a better idea of the qualities of a short story or a fable than it can of those of longer works. Yet in his longer works also Theodore's humour and irony and fantasy and wisdom and religion can strike with instant force as well as with cumulative effect. *Mr. Weston's Good Wine* and *Unclay* are quite long novels, but many passages apt for quotation will occur to their lovers. Especially, perhaps, passages from the chapters of *Mr. Weston* called " Mr. Bunce is insulted " and " Mr. Grunter steals a shilling ", and " A Drink of Deadly Wine ", where Mr. Weston gives his dark wine to Mr. Grobe. Or from the conversations between John Death and the various characters of *Unclay*. Admirers of *Mark Only* might wish Theodore to be illustrated by his description of the death of Mark; and many others would choose much else. There are scores of passages in which the more characteristic of Theodore's qualities would appear as clearly as they do in these illustrations of him from the Fable called " *John Pardy and the Waves* ":

" There was a fresh wind blowing when John Pardy reached the sea. The sun sparkled and shone upon the blue waters, and John sat himself down upon the cool pebbles within a yard or two of the waves.

" He had counted fifteen hundred—the same magic number that the angel reached to when he measured with his rod the city of the Lamb—when a very strange thing happened. The waves began to speak. Not each one of them, but they all seemed to speak together with one voice, and what they said was no easy matter for John to understand, for their words were very like their usual noise and splashing. But John Pardy, who had a quick wit, was soon able to pick out what they said.

" At first the waves spoke a little angrily, as if they were displeased at John's compliment in trying to count them."

But John Pardy assures them that he had first thought of counting the rats.

" ' Do not mention them,' said the waves, ' but, as you have set yourself so large a task, we have no objection to talk with you for a little. . . . We have lived, Mr. Pardy, for so long in our own eternal beauty, we have rocked for years without number the towering icebergs and the great ships, we have made sport for the sea-serpent and the monstrous whales, and we have rolled lazily in the wide empty spaces where God lives. We have spoken to Him, and now we are willing enough to talk to you. Indeed, we are not ashamed to say that we have often felt, even in God's company, both sad and lonely, so that sometimes we have crept inshore to see what was a-doing, approaching the shallows of the Bay of Weyminster in little inquisitive wavelets. There we have made merry with the bare feet of children, the rinds of bananas and the little paper tickets that are given to the holiday makers who hire the summer chairs.' "

John Pardy asks the waves questions about his brothers and sister, and is answered.

" ' Who would have believed it? ' he called out, ' that fifteen hundred waves, who have talked with God, should take so great notice of our little family! ' "

Then there is the Fable of *John Told and the Worm*—the gentle, philosophic glow-worm whom the gross and greedy farmer, representing the World and the Flesh, holds in his hand and means to destroy. She, the worm, attempts to convert the farmer and to save her own life.

" As she belonged to a family blessed by God with a light in the darkness, she did not wish even a man to be lost in the folly of his manners.

" ' I could tell you some wonderful things,' she said wistfully.

" ' Do not be too long,' replied the farmer, with a grin, ' in telling them, for I have heard it said that the worms devour the tender stalks of the wheat. . . . It's a pleasant thing to hold an enemy in one's grasp, and as soon as I am rested I will place you in the path, and the light you boast of will guide my boot so that I can trample you to death.'

" When she heard this sentence pronounced upon her, the glow-worm remained pensive for a while, but even then she did not lose heart nor did she despair of escaping, though she remained in the farmer's hand.

" ' Have you never thought, Squire Told,' she began gently, ' that, even if we exempt virtue and goodness, there are in the world other pleasant things more delightful than a mere possession of goods? Is there not the exquisite joy that beauty yields to its votaries, for who would wish his thought, upon such a night as this, to be occupied with the price of pork, with the manuring of a turnip field, or the killing of a little worm? How much better to contemplate the divine loveliness of the summer stars! Look upward and behold the glittering heavens! Does not such a sight awake in your mind a state of blessedness? Notice, too, I pray you, that heavy mass of blackness that is Madder Hill; see how it is set against the midnight sky. Does not the profound darkness of the hill suit the mild and deep melancholy that can join the Creator to the creature in one large sorrow? Hark you, listen to that distant sound, that heavy fall of the sea upon the summer beach! Think of the cool shining of the pebbles and the white loneliness of the great cliffs. Consider the eternal, the everlasting look of the sea itself.

Think again, Mr. Told, for a moment, upon a white daytime flower. You should know all love and sorrow when you see a meek daisy. . . .

" ' But if sublime loveliness will not enthrall you, consider the mystic longings of religion, consider the hope of eternal bliss that is promised to the merciful and to the loving. Do but allow me, Master Told, to creep safely into the grass, for indeed I promise you that none of us will ever leave this bank to rob your fields. Let me go—consider the beauty of mercy and your reward will be in heaven.'

" The glow-worm trembled, its light shone dim; but the farmer laughed heartily.

" ' The pox take your beauty,' he replied. ' I care not a fig for it. As to religion, I sit in the front pew at church, and you may be sure that a rich man who is respected here will be respected elsewhere too. God is no fool. He would never have made the earth for the rich and heaven only for the poor. What is His will in one place is His will in another. But come, it's time for me to be going. Let me squeeze out your blood upon the road.'

" ' Stay one moment,' cried the subtle glow-worm; ' if neither goodness nor virtue can please you, perhaps you may heed the voice of envy. Listen to me! Last year your wheat crop was very poor; you had only three small stacks from two great fields. . . . Now look across the way —there are five great stacks of Farmer Lord's. . . . Set them on fire.'

" 'I would gladly do so,' replied John Told, ' only I fear that the insurance company would pay neighbour Lord a larger sum than the corn would yield were it left standing. But now, hark'ee, come,' exclaimed the farmer with a chuckle, ' let me kill you, kindly.'

" ' A minute's grace I pray you to give me,' cried the worm, ' and then you may destroy me. . . . Listen! Those light steps that you hear now are the steps of a young woman. . . . Pretty Nancy Squibb is returning late and alone. . . . She is coming this way. Her blood is warmed by the excitement of dancing at the fair—she is disappointed that all was over so soon. You have but to speak. . . . Here she comes! '

" Farmer Told dropped the worm and rose hurriedly, and the glow-worm slipped into the grass and was gone."

One of the stories in a recent collection is called *Circe Truggin*. No one but Theodore Powys could have thought of such a name, one so suggestive of fantasy and magic, and of the common earth. *People Want Their Groceries* is the title of another story in this volume, and I doubt if anyone else would have thought of that either.

The invariable effect upon me of reading Theodore Powys is that I forget that I have ever suspected myself of personal bias in his favour as a writer. Together " We have heard the chimes of midnight," as he once to my joy reminded me, but even if we had never met I should, I am sure of it, feel wholly convinced that he will last as long as William Blake and John Donne.

LLEWELYN POWYS

LLEWELYN POWYS, the youngest of these three brothers, was the one that I met last. It was in 1903, more than three years after I came to know Theodore and more than two years after I first met John. Llewelyn was in his first year at Cambridge; I was in my second. My friendship with Llewelyn was always very different from my friendship with either John or Theodore, because I met Llewelyn when I was less immature, and older than he was by two and a half years. I certainly never influenced Theodore or John; but Llewelyn has said that I influenced him—" emancipated " or helped to " emancipate " him—though I feel that he would have developed as he did, and written as he did, whatever the influences on his youth; and this is what I feel too about all the members of this Powys family.

Llewelyn's influence upon me was one of the strongest and most lasting that I have known. During those Cambridge days his influence was almost wholly that of his personality, as opposed to the influence that comes from the communication of ideas. Naturally, as he was only nineteen when we met. And his mental development was the reverse of precocious, it was gradual; he often said that at Cambridge he was " a dunce ", and the Cambridge examiners may have thought so too, as they ploughed him in the Historical Tripos. He had as a youth none of the qualities of the prize-winner or the even moderately successful scholar, though by determined application he developed some of them later as is evident from his writings on literary and historical figures, especially from his book on Henry Hudson. But as an undergraduate and for some time afterwards he did not know how to set to work and he was surprisingly ignorant of many things commonly known. He had never heard of Balmoral—" God! I wish I hadn't! " was Bernard O'Neill's comment on that—and, in Venice at the age of twenty-seven, confronted by a Tintoretto picture of the Assumption, he exclaimed in amazement: " But it's a woman! " The Ascension he knew of, and thought " Assumption " must be another name for it. I remember John teasing him about Zola: " What? You don't know about *her*? Napoleon's last mistress, an enchanting one but most exacting: in fact, it was all her fault that he was so much off colour before Waterloo." But this queer, unexpected ignorance of matters of common knowledge is a Powys characteristic and John had it too. " Do you think it's warm enough in this room? " he asked me once. I looked at the thermometer and told him it was sixty. " What on earth do you mean? " he replied, with a look of bewildered incomprehension. " Sixty? Sixty! Sixty what? What the devil has sixty to do with it?" Theodore had never heard the expression "pulling my leg" and used to refer to "plus fours" as "all fours".

In later life, though, Llewelyn was far from ignorant in any sense. He came to know a good deal about the world. He was a stock-farmer with his brother Willie in British East Africa, he visited the United States, he travelled a good deal in Europe. He read widely, he meditated much, he might almost have been called erudite. But he himself, like his brothers, was always essentially the same, intact all through his life. It is not what he has learnt, it is his personality, so luminously reflected in his writings, that gives them their value.

Nearly all of the many Powyses have charm, but Llewelyn abounded in it incomparably. His smile alone, with its broad sudden light, was enough to win the stoniest heart. His radiance and warmth were in those early days something wholly new to me; they were and they remained entrancing. The young Llewelyn, with his crisp curly bright hair and fair complexion, had a sunlike look; he was dazzlingly bright. He had light eyes, eager and easily troubled, a rich unguarded mouth, a child's soft mouth greedy of pleasure and sometimes sulky. His body was hard and slight, with a hint of frailness, though one could not, then, have anticipated that he was to be so soon consumptive. He had an unusually large head which seemed even larger than it was because of its stiff woolly growth of light gold curls. It was like a growth of the earth, " crisp as a thicket of thorns ": like a vegetable growth, stiff and resilient to the touch as dry moss is in summer, or a cypress hedge. He had an air of woodland simplicity and artlessness that he never wholly lost, although later, when he knew more of the world, he could be as full of what he called " guile " as the craftiest of all those innumerable animals that he has invoked in his writings for metaphor or simile. The impression of naïvety that he still sometimes gave in his later youth and middle age was apt to be misleading. In his earlier youth he was inwardly as well as outwardly naïve: he was as much unlessoned, as much of a " dunce " in pretence or disguise or manœuvre as he was in examination knowledge or general knowledge.

I remember the shock, the momentary shock, of his instant, uninhibited expression of his feelings about two fortunate things that happened to me at Cambridge. John Powys got me a lecturing job in America and my godmother left me a thousand pounds. Both these strokes of luck pained Llewelyn. " It *is* good of Jack! " he exclaimed in wistful regret; and I can never forget his look of heartbroken surprise and indignation when I told him about the thousand pounds. Utter glumness succeeded his indignation. After the first shock I laughed with amusement and delight, and loved him all the more, because that innocent candour was so exactly like him. It was perfectly natural that he, a young man whose career was not yet determined and who had no money of his own, should suffer pangs at the good fortune of his friend. What was so engaging was the ingenuousness that made him show that he did. This was Powysian, as was the lack of worldly sophistication that he showed in those other ways. It was an expression, personal to Llewelyn, of a family characteristic. Their father, during his interviews with his lawyer, invariably sat upon his strong-box; and Theodore really did believe that the hearty appetites of his younger sisters would very soon result in the complete extinction of his own inheritance. This naïvety, in union with the partly romantic, partly morbid imagination inherited from their mother, could affect some of the Powys sons queerly. There was no suspicion, no worry, no superstition, no fantasy whatsoever, too grotesque to cast its anchor in the mind of either Theodore, Llewelyn, or John.

From our first meeting Llewelyn and I were together almost every day, going for long walks, as far even as Ely, quarrelling sometimes, when we would violently tussle and wrestle, each in anger inflicting on the other physical pain. For some while everyone but Llewelyn seemed to me irrelevant and dull. "What days those were, what days!" Llewelyn would remind me. "Can we ever forget them? Not a moment of tedium, each hour so new, so exciting. What savour, what zest!" I found every perception, every appreciation and emotion, heightened by the presence and the talk of this new and lovely friend. It was something of the same kind of intensification that I had had a year and a half before from John Cowper, but my times with John had been few and comparatively short. What Llewelyn gave me so fully day after day came much closer to me, was much more personally emotional, drove, I might say, much nearer to my heart.

My friendship with Llewelyn was in its beginnings romantic, and indeed there was always something romantic about it. It was the kind of friendship sometimes enjoyed by men, and women too, who are not homosexual but who, endowed with something of the awareness of the artist and the ardour of the poet, are drawn lovingly by the physical idiosyncrasies of the people of whom they are fond. The physical expressions of a friend's nature, the physical conveyances of a friend's charm mean more to them than they do to others; they are more deeply and more movingly interfused with the friend's self. It is possible for one man to be preoccupied by another in loverlike fashion, as I was by Llewelyn, with that special loverlike concentration, without his being "in love" completely, without his desiring any erotic contact, as he would with a girl. There can be some, while not all, of the same elements in the love of a man for a man as there are in the love of a man for a woman.

At Cambridge, as during all the future years of our friendship, it was not only Llewelyn's love of life, his awareness and response, and his charm, that enriched me and drew me close to him, but all the other qualities of his nature. In almost all my other friends there have been certain qualities that I wished away, but it was never so with Llewelyn. Even the one quality of his that I did now and then find myself resenting a little—his occasional undue elaboration, as I thought it, of punctilio and diplomacy —even this showed as so much his own that I could not really wish it gone from him. I was influenced and drawn by the whole " corpus of his consciousness "; there was nothing about him that was not dear to me: his courage, his toughness, his misgivings, his fantastically exaggerated worries and despairs, his greediness, his sensuousness, his sensuality, and his humour. Humour, so important a binder of friendship, played a most memorable part in my friendship with Llewelyn. When I think of him, I nearly always think first of some humorous or comic incident—and how many of them there were!— that we shared. I think now of a visit of his to me in Suffolk, when we went to tea with a neighbour whose husband, according to local gossip, had been discreetly dismissed from the

Army for cowardice. Llewelyn knew of the gossip and had referred to it as we were walking to take tea at the ex-Colonel's house. We found our hostess alone, and we had been with her for only a few minutes when she began to talk, in a deep, impressive voice, of her husband's career as a soldier. " He never speaks of it himself," she said. " He is so *retiring* by nature. But," she added, " he has honourable wounds." Luckily she then left us for a little while and we were able to relieve the excruciating agony of our pent-up laughter. " ' Honourable wounds! ' " gasped Llewelyn, and he indicated with a brief, positive word where the scars would be found.

In all three brothers humour is rich and deep, as is love of Nature: but Llewelyn, more than John, much more than Theodore, found joy— a Pagan joy—in all his sensibilities and responses. His whole philosophy may be summed up in the one word, " Live! " " To be alive," he writes, " only to be alive! Here is the praise, the wonder, and the glory! " This glad reassurance about life was in constant communication from Llewelyn to me in those years of our youth. It was not only at Cambridge that I was with him, but, during vacations and after we had left Cambridge, at my home in Suffolk and at his in Somerset. After my first visit to Montacute, where the father of this family was Vicar, I was made aware of the derivations of John and Theodore and Llewelyn, and began to realize how important those derivations were.

Especially important was the determining force of the father, the Reverend Charles Francis Powys, upon the family that he had begotten. It was, indeed, " He that had made them, and not they themselves," he that had created, with the unwitting power of some dim prehistoric god, both that Powys solidarity in which the identity of each one of his children could be merged, and, no less, the identity of each one of them, so separate, so distinct in all its definitions. My early experiences as a guest at Montacute Vicarage, the only alien at that great Powys Table *surmounted by the Father*, excited and baffled me, disconcerted and embarrassed me.

That Table was a formidable phenomenon. Sitting at it, I felt perturbingly single-handed, an alien invader without the ghost of a chance. I felt that I belonged to an entirely different race. If I could have changed my pigmentation and the colour of my hair to something more Powys-like, I should have felt safer.

I was not only nonplussed but resentful; for there seemed something preposterous and un-allowable about this great strong thick wall of Powys solidarity, as though it stood there blasphemous against the solidarity of the human race. As " anti-social " as the family motto *Parta Tueri*.

One monstrous Powys, many but one, the one more real than the many, that was how they, or it, appeared to me when the family was assembled. My younger daughter, as a very little girl, used to speak of them collectively as "the Powys" and she spoke better than she knew. A variation of the Athanasian Creed could be written upon them. It is very important that they were brought up as members of a large family and one so remarkably united. This had the effect of walling them in from the world, of making them draw from one another and hardly at all from outside. Of Theodore it has been said that he writes as though no one had ever written before; he is even less touched by outside influence than his brothers. Yet it is Theodore who has always seemed to be also the least touched by the influence of "the Powys", to have isolated himself from it at any rate as far as he can. He would never speak of "our mother", "our father", or "Father" and "Mother", to his brothers and sisters: "Your father" was what he always said. "Your mother says we are very happy here," he once wrote to John from a seaside place when he was a child. He much dislikes the name "Powys", or so he says. I have often known him to give queer, exciting, covert intimations of a sacrilegious disloyalty towards his family— was it done in guardianship of his own identity? "My father—" he used to say, "well, of course—" and he would stop, tasting the savour of forbidden thoughts that none could ever know. Or: "My brothers—" "It's a queer place," he said of Montacute Vicarage: that was the only preparation that he gave me for my first visit. But when I saw him there later he was as much Powys as any of them, as inevitably set under the same control.

This Powys-control, this barbaric race-pride as I used to think of it, continued to rouse my resentment when I was a young man. As an undergraduate I remember writing a scurrilous anti-Powys jingle and reciting it to an audience of three or four of the brothers, shouting it at them as derisively as I could.

> " We are Powyses, don't you see?
> Powyses, *Powyses*, you and me!
> God! what a wonderful family! "

They were all pleased by it, but Theodore was not there, and he would have been pleased the best.

I have sometimes wondered whether the idiosyncrasy of being a Powys is more important in each one of the family than their individual idiosyncrasies are. A vain speculation, for it would be futile to try to assess the relative importance or validity of " the Powys " and of the separate self in each member of this family; to try to make a percentage estimate. It is enough that the importance and validity are in both: in the common root and in each separate growth.

At Montacute Vicarage things were very different when we got clear of the Table. It was the old father whose presence was especially and inevitably able to bind the family together into that potent *fascis*: when he was gone, the one Powys began to dissolve, at least somewhat, and I drew a freer breath. He hardly ever appeared except at meals and at early morning prayers. I can hear him now, reading prayers or making his own so brief and simple ones, uttering them in his kind, gentle voice, with his look of mild forbearance as though of a Christian head of a Christian family; a voice and look so shockingly belied by the wolf-like implications of his face and the grim resistant *Parta Tueri* line of his mouth. During most of the day he was in his study—" thinking he's working," Llewelyn said—or out of doors. He loved walking. His pleasure in his walks was marred only when he passed a pair of evident lovers. Then he would sigh deeply.

The moment his father disappeared, Llewelyn would lean back, rub his hands, smile enormously, and chuckle. Flushed and giggling, I felt like a moulting bird.

The first meal I had there was the worst. Mr. Powys, after long silence, addressed me with that masking benignity:

" Llewelyn tells me that he showed you our church this afternoon." He spoke slowly and clearly. " What do you think of our Montacute church? "

I endeavoured to make an intelligent and discriminating reply. I did not know that what was required was brief but unqualified praise. I struggled, used long words, grew more and more hotly confused, repeated myself, went on too long. When I had finished, the silence was terrible. Then, " We think," said Mr. Powys, " that it is a very pretty church."

This was not a good beginning. Llewelyn gulped. Turning to him, I saw his face set in the anguish of suppressed laughter. " God! " he told me afterwards, with intense delight, " you did make a bloody fool of yourself. My father isn't used to that Archangelic talk." (" Archangel " was what Theodore had named me.)

No talk, indeed, could have been simpler than that of the Powys dinner table. The father rarely used words of more than three syllables, and he preferred those of one or two. He did not know many others, nor did he wish to know them. Any language but the simplest was to him an object of suspicion and contempt. I took the cue after that first evening. I said little, and what little I did say was entirely uncomplicated.

Mrs. Powys was friendly to me, well disposed; even, in her reserved way, affectionate: chiefly, I thought, because she saw me shy and subdued. If she had seen me gay and self-assured I doubt if she would have liked me at all. She was a romantic, sensitive, melancholy and morbid woman, indeed of William Cowper's blood. It was her qualities that made her children's genius, and the qualities of her children's father that gave it power to act, and fused with it the strange cruelty by which it is so often controlled. It needed the mental masochism of the mother, the repressed ferocity of the father, to produce *Wolf Solent* or *A Glastonbury Romance*, *Mr. Tasker's Gods* or *Unclay*, *Black Laughter* or *Earth Memories*. It needed the blood of John Donne as well. Reading Theodore's and Llewelyn's books, and John Cowper's, I am never for long unconscious of the hereditary influences of Donne and Cowper, determining, as I think, so much of their romantic excess, their melancholy, their obsessions; and of Theodore's realism and irony and brutality and holiness.

Mrs. Powys had no sympathy with success. She felt distaste for—perhaps even, with secret intensity, she hated—" well-constituted " people, or even people whose health was too good. When Llewelyn developed consumption and was determined not to die of it, she was far from friendly to his insistent will. She did not like his going to Switzerland, she did not like his having so many windows open. " These young men," she said, " seem to want to live for ever." If she had realized that John was successful she would not have liked it at all. But John never gave any impression of success in the worldly sense. So she could love him without misgiving, as she loved Theodore who, until after her death, was poor and rejected by the world. Theodore and she would sit in tragic communion, silent, with touching hands, " heartbroken," as Llewelyn put it, " over nothing," but it may have been partly because Theodore's religious heresies distressed her, as he once wrote to me that he feared they did. If Llewelyn had been content to die uncomplainingly at Montacute Vicarage, without a struggle, his mother might have loved him best of all.

Not being herself a Powys, but having for so long been the wife of one and the mother of so many others, she could understand my feelings in their midst: she could sympathize with me and wish to protect me. Also, my mother was a romantic figure of her early girlhood; with her she had read poetry, with her she had first realized it. Those were the days of Mr. Powys's courtship, when he was a handsome young man in the strength and pride and ardour of his youth.

The strength and ardour of Llewelyn's youth showed no decline in his early twenties; there was no warning of what was to happen to him when he was twenty-five. It was then that he developed consumption, the cause of which may have been the hard and anxious work involved by his American lecture tour of the previous winter, both by his preparation for it and by the lecturing itself. He remained consumptive till the end of his life; for thirty years he was at war with his sickness, sometimes seeming almost to overcome it, sometimes relapsing, sometimes near to death. But he did not die of consumption: he died of a gastric illness. Llewelyn's ill health heightened his awareness of life, and his zest for it. Life, because it might desert him at any moment, was enhanced and sharpened. His love of life was, till his death, unabated. "Love every moment of life that you experience without pain" (he wrote when he was lying on his death-bed) and that was what he always had done. "Now that my hours so sharply shorten . . . I look back to the most inconsequential and accidental of them with the liveliest regret and yearning to have them again."

But in spite of this regret and yearning for past life, Llewelyn resented the attempts that were made to prolong his life at the end. These seemed to him artificial, against Nature. "They are dragging me the wrong way," he said. He wished "to be allowed to die like a follower of Epicurus". In his last letter he wrote: "I have had a happy life for half a century in sunshine."

All through his life Llewelyn's was the philosophy of Epicurus, the philosophy of the "life-accepters", of those who rejoice in the visible world and in the life of man. But he was never a heedless optimist; he was acutely aware that life has been discoloured and maimed and impoverished by the vices of men, that man has been robbed by man, in every age, of his rightful heritage. None the less he believed that sanity, goodwill, and reason will in the end prevail. In his last letter, of November, 1939, he also wrote: "I believe . . . that the present desolations will pass and you and your children will

live in a better age with simplicity and gaiety."
In that time of war he could take from Nature
reassurance, knowing that "long after the fight-
ing is over there will remain lovely rural seascape
sanctuaries to strengthen the spirits of our
children. Though the sons of destruction have
darkened life to the point of despair, yet each
spring the sea-thrift will flower and flourish."
"The natural pleasures of natural existence will
outlast all man's ingenuity, all man's vanity and
violence, and all man's wickedness. We have
not risen out of the dust to live forever in the
Devil's mouth." "Make no doubt of it," he
had written some two years earlier, "happiness
holds empire over sorrow. In the darkest
dungeons of despair it revives against odds."

Belief in and joy in life; delight, and more
than delight, ecstasy in all sensations, whether
of spirit or body, never-failing awareness and
response, this is the religious creed of Llewelyn
Powys. "The true religion is simple," he
writes. "It is to worship life, to bow down
before life . . . in jubilant acquiescence." When
he affirmed that life was abundantly worth living
under almost any conditions—"So long as a
man can put bread into his mouth, life is to be
prized"—he spoke as one whose own conditions
of life were for the most part far from what
would generally be considered good. He never
had much money, he was often poor, recognition
of his values as a writer came slowly; he was
nearly always heavily handicapped by his disease;

and his unsound digestion constantly harassed him. But so highly did he prize life that to miss a single instant of any sort of experience, to allow one moment's dullness or slackness or trivial diversion of perception seemed to him a folly and a betrayal. " Continually," he complains, " we are preoccupied with the veriest trifles. The accidents of our life! Let them be what they may! To be able to see, to hear, to smell, to taste, and to touch—there is no higher prize. Never should we look up at the sun or see a river flowing by, with the drowned hair of its green water-weeds straining for freedom, without resolving to live with a renewed dedicated eagerness." " For those of us who trust to Nature," he declared, " there is nothing to dread."

It will perhaps be because of his appreciation of life through his feeling for Nature that Llewelyn Powys will be chiefly valued by readers of future generations, who will live in a world where Nature will still exist—at least, we hope so—but where many of the concerns that occupy the minds and exercise the art of our contemporary writers will belong to the past's dead matter. In those later days there will, I believe, be no dead matter in Llewelyn's perceptions of country sights and sounds and of the life of the creatures of the countryside, perceptions so lovingly, so romantically, and yet so realistically recorded by him, and with such close care. In his Introduction to the selections which Mr. John Wallis made from his work under the title of *The Book of Days of Llewelyn Powys* there is an example—one of so many—of what his cousin Ralph Shirley called " Llewelyn's vivid observation of minutiæ ".

" The other day somebody brought me a microscope that I might examine a morsel of sun-flower pollen placed upon a slide. To see this fecund dust transformed into innumerable golden eggs, as it were golden frog-spawn from a sunshine pool, startled me wide awake."

In his book of *The Twelve Months* Llewelyn observes both precisely and imaginatively the looks of Nature as they change under the varied influences of the year's seasons. He writes of the " genial opulence " of the month of August, and of his favourite painter Breughel's picture which represents that month, and which " treats of a harvest landscape with the corn standing ready for the sickle, as it were a solid substance of golden bread! "

In the essay on a winter month he writes that " On the Dorset downs February is marked in the natural world by two happenings. In this month the ravens begin to build their nests on a well selected ledge far up above the dizzy sea cliffs. Backwards and forwards over the wide downland valleys the black ominous lovers go, creatures with undeviating flight resolutely absorbed in their own occupations, creatures with eyes and ears and nostrils flying free through the levels of the unmeasured sky. The young of their first clutch of eggs will be hatched even before the guillemots have returned to the nesting crevices on the perpendicular side of Bats Head.

" The second happening which especially tells us it is February belongs to the night. During these weeks the foxes are mating, and the dog foxes that raise their prick ears under the star-light, or feel the brambles snatch the hair out of their red jackets, no longer give utterance to their midwinter bark, harsh and husky, but instead utter calls of love, sounds that might come through a hollow fluted reed, as if the ancient hills had truly been invaded by the children of Dionysus, calling, calling to each other to come to play. The vixen's love-call has nothing classical about it. There is no yearning, no melody in her answer. It is the cry of a soul in fear, of a tortured soul utterly abandoned to a rending desire."

In the June essay—June, the month of consummation, as he calls it—there is a passage highly characteristic of Llewelyn's exalted sensuous and poetic happiness in the life of Nature: " The sap that stirred in April and ran riot in May, by midsummer has created out of the air, out of nothing, millions upon millions of new outspreading leaves. All through the winter the sun shone upon bare twigs, bare branches, bare boughs, but these are now shaded by delicate upheld hands of palest green, by living hands of marvellous fabrication, by hands that breathe and bask through the bland day-time hours, and remain during the short summer nights cool and dedicated under the dreaming stars."

Llewelyn Powys has said that " the emotions connected with love are by far the most profound that we ever experience ": and in one of his later books, *Love and Death*, he has evoked with high poetic force those " burning apparitions ", as I once heard an Irish girl call them, of passionate love between man and woman. This love is to Llewelyn something different indeed from the " gross and brutal addiction " as which it is so often presented in our contemporary novels. In Llewelyn's writings the emotions connected with love are very closely akin to the emotions connected with Nature. They have the same kind of depth, the same kind of significance. " How often have people said to me," he begins a chapter of *Love and Death*, " ' You make too much of sex. It does not play so important a part in life as you imagine.' Let no one pay a moment's attention to such opinions. . . . Sex is the pulse-beat of life. It is the root, the straight long cow-parsley root that reaches down to the antipodes and which even the dwarfs cannot pull up!" If anyone had ever told him that he made too much of Nature, he would have replied, I think, in very much the same way. In *Love and Death* there are many scenes showing his sense of this deep affinity between Nature and human passionate love. Nature is shown not merely as a background to love, the two are interfused. But the whole book must be read for the full effect of this interfusion; which is felt in the picture of the Tintinhull lanes, with their " midsummer moon lovers", and in that potent passage describing the whirling, tumbling flight of the rooks and their settling upon the tree by which the two lovers were, together.

Love of Nature as an interpreter and illuminator of human life is the motive force of Llewelyn's writing. With an ardour that he did not deny was propagandist he seeks to convert others to his sense of values drawn from Nature, to his ideal of what should, under what he thought of as natural law, be made of life upon our planet. His sympathies involved antipathies, his affirmations involved denials, his passionate loves created passionate hatreds. He did not only celebrate and praise, he detested and denounced. The " life-deniers " are the objects of his frequent and vehement attacks; the theologians and the moralists; the persecutors and the tyrants; the worldlings, those who bow before the false gods of money, of worldly success: " Personal ambition, what is it? A folly to fan the appetites of fops."

He uses invective against the enemy: " If there exists an explanation of the Universe it certainly will not be found to coincide with the complicated theological deductions of our prosperous priests. As likely as not it is a very simple explanation with a cosmic irrationality that might well be terrifying enough to a haunted horde of saucy obsequious chop-logic ground-apes!"

Llewelyn's hostilities and abhorrences were, as might have been expected, stimulated to a special intensity by the doctrines and the practices of Fascism and Nazism and Communism. The creed of " these rash, turbulent men striving after tyrannic power", as he describes the dictators, is antipodal to his own. He believes that " the quarrel between the claims of the individual and the claims of the state should always be settled in favour of the individual ". " Free and happy men and women are always law-abiding and never seditious. It is the chained dog that bites the deepest." Denunciation of totalitarian criminality is no less implicit

in the passage that follows: " There exist, however, certain fundamental principles of human
conduct that should be honoured at all times
and in all places by all men. It is important
that these basic virtues—justice, compassion,
generosity—should never lack the support of
Epicureans."

He makes also direct attacks upon the beliefs
and the conduct of those who forced on Europe
the frightful devastation of the second World
War. " These men," he writes, " are full of
malignity and would rather that all civilization
fall to pieces than live with sense and sanity."
" What a cad, what a cardinal cad Mussolini is! "
" I believe down to the marrow of my bones
that it is no use talking of human good or human
happiness until these ancient visions of savagery
have passed away like the nightmares that they
are."

As early as June, 1934, he wrote to Mrs.
Roosevelt, who had written to him about his
books, " asking her to beg the President to make
some utterance on behalf of Democracy to which
everybody of liberal opinions could rally all over
the world." Roosevelt's reply to this request is
of interest. " I, too," he wrote, " am distressed
by the shallowness of the preachings of many of
those who are high in authority. Perhaps liberal
thought will best be served by letting them rave
on for a while before we undertake a successful
counter-offensive. . . . I think I can be of most
service to the development of liberal ideas by

taking one hurdle at a time. I am enclosing a copy of a message which I sent to Congress a few days ago and I hope you will like it."

" I hope I shall live long enough," Llewelyn wrote in 1935, " to see the fall of the tyrants."

It is evident from his published letters, from which I have been quoting, that he was much preoccupied with European dangers, from 1934 on. " Do not forget to read the first quarter of *Plato and Platonism* again," he wrote in another letter of 1935. " How different their life from the life cultivated in Berlin! "

After Munich he wrote: " It has been a bitter pill . . . and Hitler's speeches don't allow much room for sanguine hopes or prospects of any future that is not sanguinary. . . . However I look at the future, it does not seem reassuring until these crazy tyrants are tumbled off their perches."

Like all humanists, Llewelyn Powys had a hatred and horror of war, but he could never accept pacifist doctrines. " Nothing but force will stop force," he wrote to a pacifist friend. " The cat will torture until the mouse is black with her spittle and then will in the end *eat up all*. It is a very deep law."

During the last year or so of his life he saw more and more clearly what was coming to Europe. In April, 1939, he wrote: " Europe is now like a lion's den before the bones can be seen."

He had no illusions that it would be a quick

132

and easy war. "These Germans will do a lot
of mischief before they are run to earth. I can
only hope that out of the bloody agony men
will grow wiser and juster." "It is an old war
against oppression and despotism and the enemy
are sly and venomous. . . . It will surely be
savage war." "I believe we should have inter-
fered from the beginning. . . . I would rather
see England ruined than that she should have left
Europe to be devoured by this man-eating lion."

But he always believed in ultimate victory.
"These Germans are a gross and wicked tribe, but
they will overreach themselves in the end and . . .
will be crushed suddenly and burst asunder."

In his published letters Llewelyn appears
clearly and completely. To read the letters, to
read even a few dozen of them, is to know about
him. He is communicated by them with his own
vividness and force. In even the lightest of his
observations in these often hurriedly written
letters the tone of his voice is heard; as when
he comments on a seaside snapshot of a girl,
". . . this lovely little Rogue on Ringstead
Beach. I have seldom seen a girl who looked so
soft as silk or so full of irresponsible joy—the sap
of life—"

Of his books his own favourite was *Love and
Death*, which he calls "an imaginary autobiography". It is "a golden book of spirit and
sense". *Skin for Skin*, an autobiographical book,

and *Black Laughter*, a book deriving from his African experiences, are perhaps the most important among his earlier works; and, among his works of later date, *Dorset Essays*, *Somerset Essays*, *Earth Memories*, *Impassioned Clay*, and *Glory of Life*. Also *A Pagan's Pilgrimage* and *The Cradle of God*, records of his visit to the Holy Land. His biography has been written with care and thoroughness, with sympathy and understanding, by Malcolm Elwin.

" I think," Somerset Maugham wrote to me, after praising Llewelyn's portrait of Dr. Zenda, " that Llewelyn by living so long cheek by jowl with death, alone of them [that is, of the three brothers] learnt to be honest." Llewelyn did not agree with this, neither do I; but it is in a sense true that he is the only realist of the three, the only one whose contact with human affairs shows realization of things as they literally are, and a power of shrewd prevision arising out of that realization. Though he was, of the three, the most ailing in body, he was the toughest in mind. In his feelings and forecastings about the Second War, there is something that markedly distinguishes him from John Cowper and from Theodore Francis. Neither John nor Theodore has at all the same kind of contact with any reality; such contact is forbidden to them by their natures. It is true that John, in his book *Mortal Strife*, written during the Second War, was concerned with that formidable topic; and that, at the beginning of the First War, he wrote a book called *War and Culture*. In *Mortal Strife* the figures of Mr. Winston Churchill and of " Lord Haw-haw " are transformed into characters in one of John Cowper's novels. The achievement of both these books, as of John's other books, is almost wholly that of portrayal of the author in relation to the subject: the subject is little more than a frame for the portrait of the author. They have no hint of Llewelyn's objective apprehension of such matters.

Llewelyn was as " honest " about death as he was about love and religion and other concerns of human life. As truly as he could, he saw death with his naked eye, and he passionately rejected what he thought to be weak and futile and harmful illusions about it. Many will be more disconcerted and more offended by the way he sees and treats of death than by anything else in his writings. Even so sympathetic a judge of Llewelyn's work as his brother John deprecates his " Fixed Principle against the ancient Human Belief in Survival after Death ".

Llewelyn had no agnosticism about it. " *Nobis cum semel occidit brevis lux, Nox est perpetua una dormienda.*" His nature was too affirmative for him to be at ease or content in the agnostic twilight. Not " It may be so ", but " It is so ", or " It is not so ", was the way of his feeling.

It was natural to him either to accept or to deny, with the same passion, with almost the same exaltation in denial as in acceptance. He attacked Christianity chiefly because of its Pauline hostility to the flesh, but also because of the two central points of its positive doctrine. " There is no God," he declared: " There is no immortality." He was not a " doubter "; he was utterly sure. Because it was sure and certain, he proclaimed his faith in the complete extinction of every human individual with as strong an eloquence, as piercing a clarity as impelled the utterances of his faith in the greatest values of human life. If he had felt that there was the slightest chance of any survival for the individual after death, his lamentations for mortality would not have been as they were.

It was, of course, the very intensity of his love of life that caused this continual preoccupation with death. The one was bound up with the other. The surpassing sweetness and strangeness of the earth, of earth-life uncorrupted, of all that is revealed by our visions and sensations as human beings, all that we can take to ourselves from Nature and from our affections and from the arts—never could Llewelyn forget that all this, all beauty and joy, must be snatched from us for ever by unreprieving death. " This young and beautiful girl," he writes in an unpublished note, " only a few days ago so full of fantasies and hopes and so present in the vivid flesh, now lies in her shroud—and so it may happen to —— or to me in a week, in a month, in a year!" At the end of *Love and Death* there is that astonishingly actual scene in which Llewelyn anticipates his own death.

His only consolation against death was in the reflection that life could not mean so much, could not be so precious, if death were not sure so soon to end it, without any amends. If he had felt differently about death, Llewelyn could not have loved life quite as he did. Love of life had turned his thoughts to death, which he came to see as destroyer of what he loved: and then his certainty that this short life is the only one that we shall have made him prize it all the more. This heightened valuing of his few years defeated the pessimism that might have attended his rejection of any sort of survival. The interest, the excitement, the mystery and the glory of being alive sustained Llewelyn against the thought of the extinction that he believed to be the fate of our personal selves, of everything in us that enables us to respond to the precious stimulus of existence on earth.

Llewelyn sometimes seemed impatient and resentful of argument for "survival", and, I thought, disposed to reject, with hardly a glance, evidence that might seem to point to it or at least to some shadow of it; disposed to dismiss as nonsensical trifling any talk about contemporary psychic investigation, about telepathy or "the psychic factor", or about anything at all likely to challenge the materialistic thesis.

His brother Theodore assured me that it was
" dangerous " to talk like this with Llewelyn:
" it makes him angry." Sometimes I have
wondered if he had an unconscious fear that any
change in his vision of death would compel a
change disturbingly basic in himself, in his vision
of everything in life. Was that why he was
always so unshakably loyal to his great rejection?
Did he, profoundly, wish not to accept? But,
" Can you really think," he once said to me,
" that I would not believe in any continuance
of my life, if I possibly could? "

The only hint of intimation of immortality
that I ever had from him, and that a slight
enough one, to which he himself, it may be, paid
little heed, was in the last letter he wrote me,
two or three weeks before his death. He wrote
at five o'clock in the morning, having just waked
from a curious dream. After describing it he
relates how, at the end of the dream, he was in
a churchyard, " and stood looking at an
enormously tall fir tree, which I judged to be
twice the height of the tower. Its huge trunk,
almost naked of branches, rose dizzily into the
heavens. In my heart were vague misgivings as
to man's mortality."

But in his last essay for a periodical, published
in the *Adelphi* of December, 1939, the month in
which he died, he once again affirms his alliance
with life in correspondence with his enmity to
death. " Not at any time in my life," he writes,
" have I felt the least envy to be ' free amongst

the dead '. Always I would prefer the scurviest sort of existence . . . to this cursed future lodging ' where thunderclap was never heard '."

The story that I am now going to tell may seem to many people simply silly. I had never shared Llewelyn's certainty that death meant extinction; we had often argued about it. After his death I went to a "medium". Llewelyn was in my mind, but I had said nothing about him or indeed about anything. After the medium, in trance, had written first the abbreviated name " Lulu " by which he was always known to his family and friends, and then, later, " Powys ", I asked what his feelings had been immediately after death. " The first thing I thought," was the reply spoken by the medium, " the first thing was that the—the—" The medium stopped, sounds came from her throat with evident difficulty. " The word won't come," she said, " I can't get it," and then she made a sound like the German " Ach! " which she repeated, and she ended by saying, " The Ach— Ach—Ach— was right after all." (" The Arch-angel " was what the Powys brothers used to call me.)

I had telephoned to the London Spiritualist Alliance only a few hours before the sitting, and I was anonymous. It is remotely but only remotely possible that the medium knew me by sight, knew my nickname, knew of my friendship with Llewelyn and knew something about his scepticism; and about the character of his writings, for she had spoken, as Llewelyn, in a way that would not have been possible to any stranger to his work. A less unlikely explanation is that she had strong telepathic faculty and was tapping my unconscious as well as my conscious mind. I cannot think of any other explanation except the one which to many will seem the most unlikely, that Llewelyn Powys really did communicate with me after his death. But if some are fit to survive and some are not, Llewelyn was certainly among the fit ones.

In that *Adelphi* essay it is not his sense of death but his passion for Nature that chiefly appears, for his theme is the " Green Corners of Dorset ". He writes, as in his *Dorset Essays*, in his *Somerset Essays*, and in so many of his other books, with the same devoted and enamoured observation, the same happy excitement and wonder, of peacock butterflies, of salty samphire plants, of celandines shining like golden guineas in ditches, of sheep-washing pools and sequestered field ponds and mossy sparrow-tunnelled thatch, of stonechats perched on prickly sun-yellow gorse bushes, of the moon on the sea cliffs, and the foxes prowling in the twilight against the skyline when Weymouth Bay is lashed to fury. " The ferns are never false."

Memory of Llewelyn always comes in the end to rest on him as Nature's apostle. Ascetics and the orthodox, to whom his hedonism and paganism are alien enemies, will find in the expressions of his love and perception of Nature something that they cannot without loss reject: a testament manifold and enduring, made from the earth's life. As Nature's lover, as a being of " impassioned clay ", with the heightened sensitiveness of genius, he has stored beauty rich as earth and " wisdom simple as sunshine ". There are few gifts more precious than these, few that may so well defend us.

WILLIAM SOMERSET MAUGHAM

I MADE the acquaintance of Somerset Maugham
and of his work at the same time; when he
came to Cambridge to see his early play *A Man
of Honour* which was produced there in 1904 or
1905. It was, I think, my fellow-undergraduate
Ralph Straus who introduced me to him. Then
a little over thirty, he was not yet at all well
known as a dramatist; such reputation as he had
rested mainly upon his early realistic novel *Liza
of Lambeth*. He struck me as an unobtrusive,
rather wary, unusually good-looking man. His
visit was brief, I did not get anything more than a
superficial impression of him. With his play I
was more strongly impressed. It is—I had
almost said "it was," for today it is little
remembered—a play about a man who "does the
right thing" with calamitous consequence. It
reminded me of Ibsen, although I was very
imperfectly acquainted with Ibsen's work at the
time. *A Man of Honour* made me realize
more clearly the appeal that Ibsen's ethics had
for me.

In the spring of 1909 I was in Italy with a
friend, and we stayed in Florence, on the Lung'
Arno, with Reggie Turner and Somerset
Maugham. Turner we had met before, in
London, and it was he who had suggested that

my friend and I should lodge with him and Maugham. By 1909 Maugham was no longer little known. He was already beginning to have great success as a dramatist. I think it was in 1910 that three of his plays were running in London at the same time.

Reggie Turner was never successful. He had at that time published novels, but was much better known for having been one of Oscar Wilde's closest friends than he was for his novels. For me, entranced as I had been with Oscar in my schoolboy days, Reggie's friendship with him made him a figure of reflected glamour, a notable, an historic figure. Consequently he interested and attracted me a good deal more than Maugham did. Here was a man who had known Oscar intimately and had been with him at his death. I remembered his reply when Oscar told him that " Last night I dreamed I was at a banquet of the dead ". " I am sure," said Reggie, " you were the life and soul of the party." " That's the wittiest thing I have ever had said to me," was Oscar's comment.

Turner could and did engross me with his talk of the man whose spell he very soon fully revived: Maugham was outside the Oscarian magic circle. No wonder I was more taken up with Reggie Turner. He deserved the reputation that he always had as a charming and witty companion, and a kindly one. Whatever envy he had of Maugham was agreeably jesting, never malicious. " Ah, yes, yes, I know. He's very good, I know.

And good to be with. But not as good as Oscar. Not like Oscar. Oh, no, he'd never be like Oscar!" "Yes, we are leaving tomorrow. The distinguished playwright and the unsuccessful novelist will depart by the evening train for Paris." "It is my *second* editions that are rare," he said. He told me that he was with Oscar when he got my first letter and filled me with pride and joy when he added that "It pleased Oscar deeply".

But the attraction of Reggie Turner, during those days at Florence, did not cause me to overlook Willie Maugham, who made on me a quite differently memorable impression. At Cambridge I had admired his looks, but now I was aware of them as I had not been before. It was the special quality of the young dramatist's personal appearance that arrested me and that I valued. I remember little of what he said, except when he talked, as he did with reserved enthusiasm, about Spain, and about what he had done there: talk that made me decide to go to Spain in the following spring. What has stayed clear in my memory is the look of that unbelieving and guarded face that seemed so beautifully and smoothly, so strongly worked, as in rare ivory: that look of an ancient civilization, Orientally luxurious and wise. The dark brown eyes, congruous with his lustrous dark hair, suggested the eyes of some painted portrait. They gave that same effect of rich pigmentation in sudden contrast with skin pallor. When I last saw him they gave it still: it is something of the same effect as is seen in one or two of those portraits of young girls by Marie Laurencin that hang in the dining-room of his villa at Cap Ferrat. If I had never read a book or seen a play of his, I should be none the less convinced, remembering his looks and especially his eyes, that when he seems to be harsh and " cynical " he is really a romantic *à rebours*. It seems to me that his imperturbability, the whole quality of it, depends on there being so much behind it that can be perturbed. It is the impassivity that can come only out of a really tragic capacity to be moved and to suffer. His self-control suggests the secret battles waged against it; suggests but can never disclose them.

Reggie Turner's appearance was in marked contrast. There was no tragic intimation about him, and he was extremely and attractively ugly. His wit, chronicled, has delighted many who never met him, but how its edge was sharpened, how its bouquet was brought out, by his manner and his look, by the wary roguery of his screwed-up eye. His most usual remark seemed more distinctive and could give more pleasure than most people's happiest *mots*; as when he asked my friend and me: " Why don't you young people—shave? " or, a little later, in Paris, when he took us to dine at Voisin's: " Do you like food? " Or when I asked him which of the newer novelists he would recommend, and, after mentioning two or three, he said, with that

familiar twitch of the muscles of his cheek-bones:
" And I think *I'm* rather good."

When I was with him, again in Florence,
twenty-five years later, he was the same, even
outwardly, I thought. He stayed wonderfully
still in his period. He had all the essences of the
'nineties, perfectly preserved, but preserved in
something of his very own.

As it happened, I was to see in future years a
good deal more of Maugham than I did of
Turner. Maugham has always been considerate
and helpful to younger writers; he advised me
valuably, with criticism and encouragement,
about a play that I tried to write, and about
several of my novels, for one of which he wrote a
Preface. During the inter-war period I saw him
fairly often, and stayed with him three or four
times at his villa in the South of France. Contact
with that clear dry intelligence and wit always
refreshed me and gave zest to my appetite: a
mental dry sherry with anchovies or olives or
caviare or any of those sharply flavoured delicate
accompaniments of the Bacardi cocktails or
white Jura wine served at the Villa Mauresque.
(" I think I am rather younger than she is, even
now.")

During the decade or so before the Second War
I came to admire Maugham as I had for some
time admired his writing. His individualism,
his antinomianism, his anti-sentimentalism,

appearing with such force in him both as a person and as a writer, gave me a full satisfaction of a kind that I could not get from anyone else whom I knew or read, or whose plays I went to see. I may have somewhat overvalued him twenty or thirty years ago, in reaction to the undervaluing which was then fashionable. I remember how in those days, by comparison with Maugham, Shaw seemed to me a writer of pseudo-plays, a freak, Galsworthy a mediocrity, and Barrie a mess.

My enthusiasm for Maugham did not, however, at all affect my addiction to any of the three brothers Powys, partly, perhaps, because they were so remote from him both as persons and as writers. I never managed to arouse in Maugham anything but the faintest interest in John or Theodore or Llewelyn. I think Llewelyn, one of whose books I once sent him, was the only Powys he ever read, and with him he could find little sympathy. He knew enough about John and Theodore to know that he would not like their books if he did read them. I have often wished that he had met these brothers, and have thought that, if he had, he would have liked them and enjoyed them because of his and their humorous sense. But would Maugham's humour, in conversation, have been alien to a Powys, and the humour of a Powys alien to him? One evening at the Mauresque Maugham wanted a book to read in bed. " What a pity," he said, " that I wrote *Cakes and Ale*. It would be the very thing." That delighted me, but it is not at all in the Powys vein of humour, and it may be that none of the three brothers would have really relished it.

Only those who know Maugham very little or know his books very little will think of him as habitually grim or dour or forbidding. He can be like that, but he can have great charm, with lightness and a lively gaiety. I well remember one time in London, when he was lunching with my second wife and myself. Arnold Bennett was there too, and G. B. Stern. I have never seen Maugham so debonair and gay as on that occasion. There was certainly nothing sardonic about him then. This was a good thing for the luncheon party, especially as Bennett was not in health or spirits. His demeanour contrasted sharply with Maugham's, he seemed over-shadowed and over-burdened. His doctor was allowing him only one cigar a day and very little to drink. He took a glass of sherry, feeling that he ought not to.

" I hardly dared offer sherry to *you*," I said to G. B. Stern, remembering that she had written *Bouquet*.

"Oh, come." Bennett, sipping the wine, reassured me. "This is very good sherry." Just as he would say, when anyone depreciated another, " Oh, come, he's a good fellow."

He gave a kindly look both to the sherry and to me. He was a kind man. But Willie Maugham is just as kind, I thought, seeing how seemingly effortlessly, yet, I was sure, designedly, he was all the while redressing the balance of Bennett's gravity and preoccupation; talking lightly and humorously, even festively, to my wife and the others, while poor Bennett was talking to me, rather heavily and absently, about " Quies ", a wadding that defends the ears against noise. For seventeen years he had never slept without it, he said. With the same gravity he explained in minute detail how the stuff should be used. Maugham's conversation and the responses to it were continuing their contrasting effects as I expressed interest in " Quies " and Bennett made a note on a piece of paper, folded it neatly and put it in his pocket. It was to remind him to send me some of this wadding, which I received two days later with the same detailed instructions in his handwriting that I had already had by word of mouth.

As Bennett was leaving, Maugham, still in the same light and glancing humour, rallied him about his living in an upper-storey flat at Chiltern Court.

" How about the *plaque*, Arnold? " he said. " How will they manage about that? "

" Ah! That's all been arranged for, Willie. It's all been arranged for."

Those were the last words that I heard Arnold Bennett speak. He died a few months later. " *Quies*." That question about the *plaque* had been ominous. How odd it was that Maugham, in that auspicious mood, should have been unwittingly so sinister.

I sometimes wonder why that early play of Maugham's, *A Man of Honour*, is now so little regarded. Of course it is not nearly so expert a play as those that he wrote later, but it is a significant one. I still feel as I did when I first saw it, that it gives an important clue to its writer, stamping him as a kinsman of Ibsen more clearly than Shaw is stamped as such by any of his plays. The same kind of theme and the same kind of treatment are evident in *Smith*, in *The Circle*, in *The Moon and Sixpence*, *The Bread-winner*, *The Sacred Flame*, in *The Facts of Life*, to take only the first plays and stories that come to mind. " The Golden Rule is that there is no Golden Rule." " It is just as important to know when to break the Commandments as to know when to keep them." " Circumstances alter cases." These are the maxims that may be read in much of the work of Maugham as they may be in almost all the plays of Ibsen.

In *A Man of Honour* the chief character, the " man of honour ", observes the commandment that a man must " make an honest woman " of the girl he has " seduced ", and the results of his honourable conduct are disastrous. In *Smith* the young man looking for a wife defies the commandment not to " marry beneath " him— a social commandment overruled in the case of the man of honour by the " superior " moral one. He marries his sister's parlourmaid, and does so with the prospects of far better results than if he had married in his own class. If his behaviour is superficially viewed, it resembles that of the man of honour, for both these men marry women who are not their social equals. But the circumstances are quite different, therefore what is wrong for the one man is right for the other. In the first play the hero makes a tragic blunder by self-sacrificingly doing " the proper thing"; the hero of the second play acts wisely by not doing it, and he acts entirely in his own interest. The moral of each play is unmistakably Ibsenesque: " Beware of rules of thumb. Examine them in relation to the particular circumstances and reject them if the circumstances seem to you to demand it." Private judgment—the judgment which a man or woman of character can rightly exercise—is the wisest and best rule of conduct. This is an extreme, a " Left Wing " Protestant doctrine, a logical development from Protestant faith.

This particular moral aspect of Maugham as a writer has not, I think, been thrown often enough into clear relief. It is surely important, and it lights up other aspects of his that have been more generally noted by his readers and critics. For Maugham is a serious writer, a moral writer, strongly moved by his own rebel morality. He is a tragic writer, afflicted by human weakness, by human unhappiness, by that " human bondage " of which so much is due to human laws and codes. He is the more tragic because he has not, as Oscar Wilde had, the consolation of an irresponsible sense of comedy, nor has he Thomas

Hardy's consolations of poetry and of Nature, nor the consolation of that rich zest for existence, that " life-acceptance " which perhaps only those who possess the poetic sense can fully enjoy.

Even those characters of Maugham's who are shown as rightly and to some extent successfully breaking the law, even those who most nearly triumphantly vindicate individualistic doctrine in Maugham's fiction, are not really triumphant. No word, indeed, could be less appropriate to the ultimate sense and feeling, to the upshot of any play or story that Maugham has written than any word like " triumph ". It is better than if the man, or the woman, had done the other thing: that is the most one can say. In *The Circle*, as the last curtain drops, there echoes in our ears the unconsciously ironical laughter of the old man who, having blundered, believes that he has been extremely clever, and the consciously ironical laughter of the others as they hear the " downy old bird's " self-congratulations. This is our last impression, so characteristic of this writer, an impression of human folly and of the comic irony that may make us some amends by being brought to play about it. As to the eloping Elizabeth and her paramour, they are in the right, they justify the doctrine of Maugham and of Ibsen that " what matters is what you are, not what you do ". It was a mistake for the other couple, for Lord Porteous and Lady Kitty to elope—or, rather, it was more damaging in the long run to their well-being for them to do so than it would have been for Lady Kitty to have stayed with her husband. But, as Elizabeth and her lover are quite a different sort of couple and their circumstances quite different, it will damage their well-being less if they go off to Malaya together than if they give each other up. Elizabeth is very clearly informed by her young man that he does not offer happiness to her. The love that he offers is worth—or may be worth—the price she will have to pay for it. In any case, she must accept, she must pay; because of her nature, and because of his, she " can no other ". There is nothing for it, under the circumstances, but adultery.

A different commandment is broken by the mother in *The Sacred Flame*. She kills her son, knowing that it will be the worse for him if she doesn't; and the worse for her, too, for she, devoted to him, will have to witness his utter, incurable misery and devastation. He is the victim of a flying accident, legless and impotent, wholly dependent in loving faith upon his wife: when he finds her out, as he must, he will be slowly and excruciatingly tortured to death. His mother knows this and she gives him a fatal dose of his sleeping-draught. She is right, things being as they are, but neither she nor anyone else has cause for exultation. For this reason, too, we are reminded of Ibsen's plays.

" That man most nobly lives and nobly dies Who keeps the laws himself has made," or something like it, was written by Richard Burton; and in those lines is the kind of exultation that is not to be found in the work of Maugham, who thinks exactly the same. Again and again, in his plays and short stories and novels, unhappiness, relieved by irony, is in the end dominant; most notably, perhaps, in *Of Human Bondage*, the first book of his to gain him what might be called a literary reputation, and certainly one of the unhappiest tales that he ever told. But in *The Moon and Sixpence* and in *The Breadwinner*, although the conduct of Strickland and of the other stockbroker husband and father undoubtedly caused their commonplace and unadmirable families discomfort and some minor unhappiness, the stories are not tragic or in the main even unhappy. They are ironical, of course, or they would not be Maugham's, but the irony is of a milder sort, as in the accounts given of the attempt to bring Strickland to a sense of his duty soon after his flight to Paris, and of the biography of him written by his clergyman son. Strickland, however, is more nearly triumphant than any of Maugham's heroes: at any rate his art triumphs in being brought to life and to achievement and in its so complete justification of his desertion of his family. The " bread-winner " is quite another case. He is an average man, his only distinction being that he has the moral courage to live the life he wants to live, which is not the life of a stockbroker bound daily to his office so that he may provide gentility and comfort for his wife and children, but the life of a rentier travelling abroad and seeing the world in a modest way on a part of the money that he reserves for himself from his capital, while his family live, much more modestly than they care to, on the larger part reserved for them. The bread-winner is nothing like so unscrupulous as Strickland, he has not the same reason to be so and he is a " decent fellow "; but he is condemned by the public opinion of the world he lives in as a scoundrel or a lunatic, or both. No one can understand the " rider " that he makes on Ibsen's doctrine that " a woman has the right to live her own life, to realize herself ": " If a woman, then why not a man? " Just as Nora Helmer would have been understood or even condoned if she had left her husband and children for another man, so the bread-winner would have been understood, he would have found some furtive sympathy, if he had left his family for another woman. And the same applies of course to the hero of *The Moon and Sixpence*, notwithstanding the difference of his motives and his character. It is a Strindberg inversion of Ibsen that appears here too.

The Facts of Life is the lightest in treatment and in substance of all Maugham's distinctively Ibsenesque works of fiction. A youth defies his father's wise advice: he gambles, he gets mixed up with a loose woman, he lends money, and these adventures bring him nothing but pleasure and profit. He comes out top, everything ends most agreeably and amusingly, but " triumphantly " would be too strong a word for it. The boy is, rather, " cock-a-hoop ", and well he may be.

No less than Shaw, then, certainly no less though very differently, may Maugham be said to be in the tradition of the great Norwegian dramatist; but of course such a discipleship or heritage, interesting and significant though it is, would not by itself have brought either Shaw or Maugham his fame. *A Man of Honour*, though deriving so clearly from Ibsen, did not succeed because it had no more than a small measure of those other qualities for which Maugham's later plays are distinguished. It had not wit enough, nor a sharp enough irony, nor enough force of dramatic effect. It is an able play, not a brilliant one: it might even be classed among the better of those dull, able plays not infrequently to be seen in experimental theatres. And Ibsen's doctrine is not in itself generally acceptable; it needs high excellences of dramatic art and of irony or wit to make its presentment palatable to most play-goers or readers of fiction. The average man or woman does not break the commandments, or breaks them at the wrong time and with the wrong results: he or she does not like to be reminded of that, and those who are more weak than strong (the majority) are likely to be intensely irritated by propaganda for an indi-vidualist " anarchy " upon which only the strong can rightly act.

When he wrote *A Man of Honour* Maugham had not developed his powers, so he could not " get

away with " a play on such a theme. He is not
what is called " a born writer ": " a made
writer " is what he has called himself. His early
work—even *Liza of Lambeth* and certainly the
books of the period of *The Merry-go-Round*—has
little or nothing to distinguish it from the
forgotten work of many other writers of that
time. Later, when he began to write well, the
critics were unfair to him for two reasons: they
were prejudiced by their memories of his early
faults and, more importantly, they did not want
to believe that a writer of such popular plays
could possibly have any literary merit. He must
be making a lot of money, he could not be anything but a cheap-jack. This was Maugham's
second phase; the phase of his first success as a
playwright, the time when he became well
known, and it was also the time when the critics
contemptuously described his work as " near-
beer ", or, if they knew enough French, as
" *faux-bon* ". His style, they said, was un-
distinguished, his characterization superficial, he
was cheaply cynical and he was unduly preoccupied by sex.

Such depreciation of Maugham in orthodox
literary circles continued even after the publication of *Of Human Bondage* some six years later, in
1915. It was " as much as one's literary life was
worth ", even during most of the inter-war
period, to praise Maugham's writings. In a
comparatively recent book—I think *The Summing
Up*—Maugham has good-humouredly observed

that clever young men don't write essays about him. There is this, however, to be said in apology for his depreciatory critics: Maugham as a playwright had deliberately given the public what they wanted at the end of the first decade of the century—light, amusing, epigrammatic, trivial comedies, rather French, with a touch of the manner of Wilde. He wanted to establish himself, to get known and to get the money that he needed so that he could be free to write as he wanted to write. " I'll give them what they want now," he is reported to have said, " but, when I can, I'll write to please myself and then I'll let them have it! " Perhaps he never said anything of the sort; but the words are prophetic of the cat-calls and booing that broke from resentful members of the audience when *The Circle* was put on many years later.

Maugham is now seventy-eight, and after the age of seventy every English writer, who has written enough, automatically becomes respectable. He is then respected for his achievement and forgiven for whatever offences he may have committed against the proprieties, against " good taste ", or against orthodoxy of any kind. Maugham has now lived down the offence that he gave by what appeared as such distasteful blemishes or indiscretions to the critics and readers of past years. He is no longer rebuked for cynicism, for unromantic and discomfiting treatment of women and of the sexual impulse; and the highbrows have forgiven him for having made so much money. His material success, since it started about forty years ago, no longer means that he must be an inferior writer.

Another reason for the general acceptance of Maugham today as the *doyen* of English writers—occupant of the place that his Alroy Kear so earnestly craved in *Cakes and Ale*—is that the many-sidedness and the pattern of his work have naturally become more and more evident as he has written more and more. Nearly thirty years ago he wrote to me that the observation made by one critic that "There are as many Mr. Maughams as there are books he has written" had pleased him (" perhaps foolishly," he added) more than anything else that had been said about him. At the same time he told me that he had in his mind a pattern which he hoped to complete if he lived long enough; which means that no one of his books was written in isolation, but as contributory to that pattern, which is now, but could not be before, visible as a whole. In earlier days it could only be guessed at. A pattern of variety designed for its total effect.

What is posterity likely to think of that pattern and of its components? Will Somerset Maugham be some part of the life of the future? That is, will he enter into the lives of unborn readers, whether of many or few in each successive generation, as the greater writers of the past enter into our lives? No writer can do this unless, by virtue of his vision of life and his power of expressing it, he gives something that no one else can. The purely popular dramatists and story-tellers may win contemporary fame and so may second-rate or third-rate writers of recognized " literary merit "; but, after they are dead, other writers of equal facility or talent will oust them because they will satisfy much better the changed tastes, highbrow or lowbrow, of their period. What keeps writing alive is not necessarily those qualities that were chiefly responsible for its appeal to the public that first acclaimed it. An author may lack any real strength of separate identity and may yet, for one accidental reason or another, be eminently successful in his own day. But if he has his own separate feeling for human tragedy or comedy, for the passions, for character, or for Nature; if he has his own poetry or irony or wit or humour, if he has originality in depth, no matter with what trend or bias, then he will continue to be of interest. He will have a tested value and will become a " classic ", if no more than a minor classic like Suckling, Beddoes, or Smollett, supposing that he has limited scope.

It may be that Maugham would himself deprecate any claim upon posterity. Another reported saying of his is that he was under no illusions about his position as a writer: " I know just where I stand: in the very front row of the second-rate ones." Also that " I haven't more talent than the next man, but I have more character ". Whether or not Maugham denies that he possesses exceptional talent, he is not anxious to be described as a man of genius. Once, when a young admirer had been eulogizing him to his face and saying a good many things about his " genius ", the unresponsive looks of his host gave him pause, and then, more warily, he said something about "craftsmanship". " ' Craftsmanship '," Maugham repeated, " yes, that's more like it." For this I can vouch as I was there.

Readers of the future will be better able to judge whether or not Maugham has genius, and their judgments may vary as posterity's judgments sometimes do. But it may be said now and with some conviction that, if Maugham does think himself a second-rate writer with no unusual talent, if he thinks himself a mere craftsman, he is wrong. The individual quality of his best work is unmistakable; no one else could have written it. It is recognizable as his by a para-graph, even sometimes by a sentence. His ironic effects are especially unmistakable; they are different from those of any other writer because they are led up to in a different way, and, when they come, they come communicated with the very tone of their contriver. Nor is his sense of tragedy less his own inalienable property. It is tragedy that is not redeemed or purged by poetry, it has no heightening and brings no liberation: it is sheer unhappiness, sheer loss; it is, in fact, tragedy as most men and women know it, but is there any other living English writer who has shown the same sense of this usual kind of misery? Writers of other countries and of past generations come to mind—de Maupassant, Gissing—but their vision is different, they give different effects. In *The Painted Veil*—though this is not one of his best books—the wretchedness of Kitty remains unforgettable because the sense of it is stamped with Maugham's identity; and the sorrow of Mrs. Hamlyn in the short story called *P. & O.* stays in the memory for the same reason, so do the anguish and frustration of Eva in *For Services Rendered*.

Like some other writers of exceptional faculties, Maugham is able to identify himself with his women characters and, discarding male tolerance of women's faults, he does this with an effect that used to shock people who prided themselves on their chivalrous regard for the fair sex. The effect was likely to startle anybody, because it was new. Or, at least, Maugham's " interior " view of women was new to most earlier twentieth-century readers. He makes especially clear certain sexual realities of women and the profound differences between these realities and those of men, clashing differences inevitably involving antagonisms, so that women and men, seen under this light as animals of two different species, must become enemies. Other writers have exhibited the same conflict, but not in Maugham's way; not with the same identification of the writer with the sexual nature of women, not with the same realistic, logical sense of all that the conflict involves. More remarkable, perhaps, than any other disclosure that Maugham makes about women is his disclosure of their physical sexual appetites, of that female lust which all respectable men in Victorian and even in Edwardian times refused to believe had any existence. There is, surely, no English contemporary writer who gives quite the same impression of inside information on this matter as Maugham does, who is able to convince us in the same way that this is really how women feel when they are under erotic stress, differentiating their feelings so sharply from the feelings of men in the same case: and the reason why he convinces thus is because he seems to be writing not from the observation that a man might make in experience with a responsive woman, but from the experience of the woman herself. He seems to possess the special knowledge of the gynecologist, a gynecologist who has the rare ability to, as it were, " become " his patients. Maugham's medical training and practice may partly account for his intimacy with the feelings of women as it may partly account for his psychological observation in general. As with Chehov and Schnitzler we often feel that it is a doctor's observation, professional, experienced, and seemingly callous, of human nature, male and female.

Another reason why Maugham's intimations of the erotic emotions of women are so unlike the usual intimations given in plays and novels is that he almost as rarely allows himself to be romantic as he allows himself to be sentimental: with the result that neither romantic nor sentimental glamour interferes with physical realities either by heightening them or by falsifying them. Even Elizabeth in *The Circle* is not in love in the full romantic sense; she is not a romantic girl. Nor is any one of Maugham's women romantic. They are passionate, they can be tender, or they can be sentimental with their sentimentalism satirically viewed, but there is no authentic poetry in them, they do not " smite the high chill air with flame ".

It used to be—perhaps it still is—a fairly common complaint against Maugham that he does not appreciate the better qualities of women; that he presents women as callous, brutal, selfish, vain, silly, trivial, mendacious and unscrupulous. (" Not more unscrupulous than most women," Lady George in *Our Betters* defends herself.) There is no doubt that he does present such women, no doubt that he is what is called " disillusioned " about the sex. But few better, more unselfish—or, indeed, more saintly— women can be found in modern fiction than the nuns in *The Painted Veil* and they are not the only good women depicted by this writer. There is Mrs. Ardsley in *For Services Rendered*, that good woman who is also a woman of good sense, of strength of character, and of fortitude, which Maugham prizes perhaps more highly than any other virtue. There is the mother in *The Sacred Flame*, there are minor characters such as Mrs. Hamlyn, and there is Rosie in *Cakes and Ale*, Rosie the most attractive and the most refreshing of all Maugham's women, a comedy figure but an intrinsically good woman none the less, one of those whom one would wish multiplied through every country so as to make the world a happier place. Kitty in *The Painted Veil*, Leslie in *The Letter* are by no means wholly good or admirable women; but they are portrayed with humane sympathy as well as with understanding, especially Kitty in the later part of the book.

Maugham, like Joseph Conrad, shows strong distaste for much that is to be found in Western life and ideas and standards; European and American women seem to him, as they did to Conrad, in many respects de-feminized and therefore spoilt: inferior, in certain essential qualities, to the women of the East who not only make their men happier but are happier themselves, less discontented, even under what seem to us to be very bad conditions of life, because their basic demands as women are satisfied. Maugham's affinity with Eastern thought and with the Eastern way of life is clearly enough shown in many of his later stories and in his play *East of Suez*. It has been recently said that he is part hermit and part man of the world. Perhaps the reason for this is that as a writer of fiction he has had to be concerned with a world that on the whole he dislikes: while taking part in the life of this Western world, while moving in it and observing it, even while being greatly interested in it, he has had the evident impulse to escape.

His preoccupation with and attraction to Eastern philosophy and religion appeared as unexpectedly, even startlingly strong in *The Razor's Edge*, a book that must have caused some revision of the opinion of those who had persisted in believing him a complete materialist. In his earlier days he may have been that; but his later and long continued Eastern contacts, his increasing awareness of Eastern spiritual thought and practice, could hardly have failed to challenge his materialism and, at the very least, to modify it. Ten years or more before he wrote *The Razor's Edge* he had written *Sheppey*, and that play is based upon a strong sense of spiritual values. Sheppey, trying to be a literal Christian, is overcome by the world, but he saves his soul. Maugham has said that *For Services Rendered* is his only propagandist play, and it is the only play of his that bears evident marks, indeed too evident, of propagandist intention and design. But in a broader or looser sense many of his plays are propagandist, and surely *Sheppey* may be considered as propaganda against Western materialism.

Formerly current criticisms of Maugham can hardly, therefore, carry the weight that once they seemed to carry. To anyone who knows his work as a whole he cannot now appear as a woman-hater, a brutal cynic, a sufferer from sex-obsession, a drear materialist. Nor does he appear as nothing more than an exceptionally clever craftsman in the arts of the novel and play and short story. It was perhaps his craftsmanship almost as much as his success that prejudiced former critics against giving him the distinguished place that he has long since deserved in contemporary literature. He was too good a craftsman, they seem to have thought, to be anything more. It was easy to dismiss him (as he has seemed modestly disposed to dismiss himself) to that lower rank, with perhaps some justifying reflections upon his remoteness from those wayward, faulty, blundering men of genius in whose " vexed beating stuffed and stopped-up brain there burns a truer light of God . . . than goes on to prompt This low-pulsed forthright craftsman's hand. . . ."

A quite recent criticism of Maugham is one that has more substance. It has been said that he defaces his writing with " clichés ", that he is more and more exclusively concerned with the execution of his story and with its consequent effect; that he is becoming more and more commonplace in his phraseology and in his style. In or behind this there is some truth, although Maugham has again and again shown and continues to show that he is capable of a drastic pungency of expression that is very much his own. But he has always fought shy of literary mannerisms, was always on his guard against " fine writing ", has always taken care not to ride the literary high-horse. When he began to write, preciousness, literary affectation, decorativeness, style with a good deal of nonsense about it, were special dangers for young writers. (" Should power of inspiration from Parnassus' heights be esteemed as sole criterion, then were the Laureate Crown for Mr. Swinburne's head alone. But a republican singer could hardly, with grace, wear a Crown Queen-given.") Young writers, trying to copy Wilde and Pater, often made fools of themselves; and Maugham would, I think, have always been very much alive to the risk of ridicule on the score of pretentious or pseudo-poetical writing. His preference for Hazlitt as opposed to Lamb or to de Quincey is significant. Then, again, he is a playwright, and it is impossible for a playwright to give the impression of reality unless he makes his characters talk in an ordinary way, using a certain number of " clichés ". This is also true of the novelist, but dialogue is not the greater part of a novelist's work, so he does not get so much into the habit as the playwright does of writing down trite expressions which may affect his own style.

That Maugham, like everyone else, has the defects of his qualities no one, least of all himself, would want to deny. His occasional flatness is the defect of his great virtue of economy, of despatch. His " dryness " cuts both ways. He is so restrained and so well disciplined that we may find ourselves wishing that he would some-times let himself go for a change. But no criticism can be more unfair or impertinent than criticism of a writer of notable qualities for his deficiency in qualities that it is not in his nature to possess. This is criticism of him for not being another kind of writer. Maugham is not a stylist nor a romantic; sometimes, because of a lack of zest and sap, he would seem to " write down " life, to take a lower view of it than the life-lover would think justified; his relish, his amusement, are nearly always oddly reticent and subdued; nor is there eloquence in his writings, certainly not that poetic eloquence with its magical, strange release and overflow. In a sense he may be called " earth-bound ", although not only *The Razor's Edge* and *Sheppey* but other indications scattered through his work are a warning against the use of such a word without important reservations. What is certain is that he could have attained neither his reputation nor his popularity—it means a great deal when a disillusioned and " depressing " writer comes to be widely read—if it had not been for his firm possession of the much more than compensating qualities of his defects. He is not only a crafts-man of surpassing excellence, both as playwright and as novelist, and a master of the short story;

169

he is a realist with his own barb, an ironist with his own " tragic terseness " and with his own feeling for comedy; he has wit of his own, humour of his own, and his own veracity in portraying character; and he is among the most cogent individualists of our time, one who has modernized the doctrine of Ibsen and given it a new force.

THE END

MADE AND PRINTED IN GREAT BRITAIN
AT THE CHAPEL RIVER PRESS
ANDOVER, HANTS
11.52